MEALS FOR
Good Health

By Karen M. Graham
Registered Dietitian (R.D.)
Certified Diabetes Educator (C.D.E.)

To my many clients over the years
who were my inspiration
to write this book.

 PAPER BIRCH PUBLISHING
89 Wilkinson Crescent
Portage la Prairie, Manitoba R1N 1A7 Canada
Email: pbp@mealsforgoodhealth.com

**For information about *Meals for Good Health* and other
nutrition resources such as the *Meals for Good Health*
CD and DVD, visit www.mealsforgoodhealth.com or call the
publisher at 1-204-857-7365. To place an order, order at
www.mealsforgoodhealth.com or contact:**

US Distributor:	Canadian Distributor:
Focus on Growth	Team Tools Ltd.
P.O. Box 312227	P.O. Box 20162
New Braunfels, Texas 78131-2227	Brandon, MB R7A 6Y8
Call toll-free: 1-800-496-8508	Call toll-free: 1-866-733-9409

Canadian Cataloguing in Publication Data
Graham, Karen, 1959-
   Meals for Good Health: low-fat, high-fiber meals
Karen Graham. -- 3rd ed.
Includes index.
ISBN 0-9696770-6-5
   1. Low-fat diet--Recipes. 2. Menus. I. Title.
RC662.G73 2005   641.5'638   C2004-907285-4

Meals for Good Health has been translated into French and is published by
Les Éditions de l'Homme in co-operation with Association Diabète Québec,
sold under the title of *La santé au menu*, ISBN 2-7619-1588-7.
Access French side of website at www.mealsforgoodhealth.com. Click on
"Meals for Good Health Resources".

EDITOR: JANICE MADILL, EASY ENGLISH
PHOTOGRAPHER: BRIAN GOULD, BRIAN GOULD PHOTOGRAPHY INC.
FOOD STYLIST: JUDY FOWLER
ORIGINAL DESIGN: DURAND & GRAHAM LTD, WITH ASSISTANCE FROM
   STEVE PENNER, FRIESENS CORPORATION
REVISION DESIGN: RACHELLE PAINCHAUD-NASH, FINE LINE DESIGN
PRINTED AND BOUND IN CANADA BY: PREMIER PRINTING LTD.

Cover photo: Tacos (page 170-173)

Words of Thanks

My thanks to all of you who use *Meals for Good Health* to achieve good health. You have told me how this book has helped you lose weight, and reduce your cholesterol, blood pressure and blood sugars. For me, as an author, there is no greater sense of satisfaction than knowing I have helped others.

My thanks also go to the organizations who, over the years, have provided support or partnership on earlier versions of *Meals for Good Health.* Special thanks to the Canadian Diabetes Association, the National Literacy Secretariat, the Lions Club of Portage la Prairie, Health Canada, the National Aboriginal Diabetes Association, and Maytag Canada. All the nutrient analyses in the book were completed by the Canadian Diabetes Association contract dietitian, Kathy Younker, and approved by the Canadian Diabetes Association.

It is true that a picture is worth a thousand words. Thank you Brian Gould and Judy Fowler, for your skill and artistic talents and for capturing exquisitely beautiful and tantalizingly realistic images.

Thank you to my sister and editor, Janice Madill; over the last ten years you have directed me with perception and wisdom. Thank you to my parents, Marg and Bill Graham, for innumerable editorial reviews, and to my brother Douglas Graham. Thank you to the dietitians who reviewed this edition or the first edition: Cynthia Abbott Hommel, Kristin Anderson, Wendy Graham, Nina Kudriakowski, Dr. Diane Morris, Gina Sunderland and Kathy Younker.

The concept for *Meals for Good Health* was born over ten years ago following brainstorming and discussions with my husband, Rick Durand. Thank you Rick for your contribution of ideas, your reviews, your humour, your daily encouragement and love—you have been instrumental at every stage. Our children, Carl and Roslyn, have grown up in the midst of the book and they themselves have become stalwart supporters and promoters of the book's concepts of healthy living—thank you for your enthusiasm and for making this adventure fun and complete.

How To Use This Book

Color coded sections of the book

> ### *White—Ideas for Healthy Living*
> - Important and practical advice to help you lose weight.
> - Changes you can make to be healthier.
> - Valuable information on how to reduce your cholesterol, blood pressure and blood sugars.

Yellow—9 Breakfast Meals
All large meals have 370 calories
All small meals have 250 calories

Green—10 Lunch Meals
All large meals have 520 calories
All small meals have 400 calories

Blue—31 Dinner Meals
All large meals have 730 calories
All small meals have 550 calories

Purple—4 Snack Groups
Low-calorie snacks have 20 calories or less
Small snacks have 50 calories
Medium snacks have 100 calories
Large snacks have 200 calories

Meals for Good Health *is a daily meal planner showing meals and snacks that total from 1200 to 2200 calories per day. Your calorie total will depend on whether you choose the large or small meals and the number of snacks.*

Meals for Good Health has life-size photographs of all the meals in the book.

Step 1: Read "Ideas for Healthy Living"
Step 2: Determine your Daily Calorie Needs
- Use the general rule
- Use your hand size, or
- Use the calorie counter

Step 3: Choose your Meal Plan
- Daily Meal Plan Chart
- Make your own meal plan

Step 4: Make the Meals and Recipes
Step 5: Add Daily Exercise
Step 6: Go to Website for Support

STEP 1
Read "Ideas for Healthy Living"

The nutrition information in this book is based on the recommendations of the *Food Guide Pyramid* and *Canada's Food Guide to Healthy Eating*.

These recommendations include:

- choose a variety of foods every day
- eat in moderation
- eat regular meals
- eat less fat
- eat more starchy foods and fruits and vegetables
- eat more high-fiber foods
- be active and feel good about yourself

STEP 2
Determine Your Daily Calorie Needs

Choose one of the following three methods:

Method 1: Use the General Rule

If you are trying to lose weight, here is a general rule:

- Women choose 1200–1800 calories daily
- Men choose 1500–2200 calories daily

Use the Daily Meal Plan Chart on page 9 to choose your meal plan.

Method 2: Use Your Hand Size

- Go to page 96–97, to the life-size photograph of Dinner 1.
- If the palm of your hand is about the size of the $1\frac{1}{2}$ chicken breasts and your fist is about the size of the $1\frac{1}{2}$ potatoes, then choose the large meals.
- If your hand is closer in size to the one piece of chicken and one potato (shown in the small inset photograph), then the small meals are for you.
- You may want to add several snacks to your daily meal plan. But if you are trying to lose weight, you may need to choose just the small snacks or the low-calorie snacks.
- Over time, based on your weight loss or gain, adjust the meal size and the number of snacks.

The portions will need to be adjusted for each member of your family. The small meals would be enough for most small children. But growing children and teenagers may need portions larger than even the large meals and large snacks. For children and teenagers, include a cup of milk with each meals to meet their calcium needs.

SMALL MEAL

The calorie counter works best for those over age 18. It will take into account your gender, age, height and physical activity. **It does not take into account:**
- *variations in body metabolism*
- *differences in bone and muscle structure*
- *the extra calories needed for growing children and teenagers, or during pregnancy and breastfeeding, or for those in high intensity exercise training.*

Method 3: Use the Calorie Counter

- The calorie counter calculates the numbers of calories you need in a day to maintain your current weight.
- It is online at www.mealsforgoodhealth.com to save you doing the math.
- Or, fill in the boxes below to calculate your daily calories.
- Once you have your daily calorie number, you can choose your meal plan. Please see Step 3 (page 9).

To lose weight:
- You need to subtract 300–500 calories from your daily total.
- A slow, gradual weight loss is best. This way you lose fat, not important muscle and water. For example, if you lose 2–4 pounds (1–2 kg) a month, you will be doing great.

Calorie counter (Write the answers in the boxes)

A. Start with this number:
387 (women)   864 (men) ....

B. Multiply your age by
7.31 (women)   9.72 (men) ....

C. Subtract line B from line A (Note: Result may be negative) ....

D. Multiply your weight in pounds by
4.91 (women)   6.39 (men) ....

E. Multiply your height in inches by
16.78 (women)   12.77 (men)....................

F. Add lines D and E ....

G. Enter your daily physical activity level:
Sedentary (no regular activity) 1.0
Low active (up to half-hour per day)
        1.14 (women)   1.12 (men)
Active (30 to 60 minutes) 1.27
Very active (over an hour)
        1.45 (women)   1.54 (men)

H. Multiply line F by line G ....

I. Add lines C and H. This is your total daily caloric maintenance level: ....

Adapted from "Dietary Reference Intakes", The Institute of Medicine, September 2002

STEP 3
Choose Your Meal Plan

A. Daily Meal Plan Chart

• small meals with no snacks	1,200 calories
• small meals with two small snacks	1,300 calories
• small meals with one small snack and two medium snacks	1,450 calories
• small meals with one small, one medium and one large snack	1,550 calories
• large meals with no snacks	1,620 calories
• large meals with two small snacks	1,720 calories
• large meals with one small and two medium snacks	1,870 calories
• large meals with one small, one medium and one large snack	1,970 calories
• large meals with three large snacks	2,220 calories

Once you have selected your meal plan, then you can mix and match your meals without ever worrying again about calories. Everything is worked out for you.

B. Make Your Own Meal Plan
Rather than using the chart, you can create your own individualized meal plan. You can mix and match different sized meals and snacks, depending on the eating schedule that best fits your lifestyle. For example:

Meal	Calories
Large breakfast	370
Small snack	50
Small lunch	400
Large snack	200
Large dinner	730
Medium snack	100
Total Calories	1850

For the small meals:

- breakfast has 250 calories
- lunch has 400 calories
- dinner has 550 calories

For the large meals:

- breakfast has 370 calories
- lunch has 520 calories
- dinner has 730 calories

For the snacks:

- low-calorie snack has 20 calories or less
- small snack has 50 calories
- medium snack has 100 calories
- large snack has 200 calories

STEP 4
Make the Meals and Recipes

About the book's 60 recipes:

- easy to make
- low-cost and use common ingredients
- low in fat, sugar or salt
- family favorites
- easy to freeze

Check the recipes for the number of servings. Some recipes will serve up to six people. If you live on your own, you may want to cut the recipes in half. If you are cooking for a large family, the recipes can be doubled. Leftovers can be safely kept in your fridge for three days, or frozen to be eaten later.

About the weights and measures used in the recipes, meals and snacks

Standard measures are used in the recipes. If you want to use metric measures, here are the changes:

1 cup (8 ounces)	=	250 milliliters (mL)
1/2 cup (4 ounces)	=	125 mL
1/3 cup (3 ounces)	=	80 mL
1/4 cup (2 ounces) (4 tablespoons)	=	60 mL
1 tablespoon (3 teaspoons)	=	15 mL
1 teaspoon	=	5 mL
1 ounce	=	28 grams
1 pound	=	454 grams

Measure your glasses & bowls.
Your drinking glasses and cereal and soup bowls may be different shapes than the ones shown in the meal photographs. Fill up a measuring cup with water and pour the water into your glasses and bowls. Then you will know how much they hold.

Choosing smaller glasses and dishes will help you reduce your portions.

STEP 5
Add Daily Exercise

It is very important to keep active. Experts recommend 30 minutes a day (or 45 to 60 minutes four times a week) of an exercise such as walking, biking or swimming. See pages 42–44 for more information about keeping active.

STEP 6
Go to Website for Support

www.mealsforgoodhealth.com

Click on the menu bars listed below.

Karen Graham, Author,
Registered Dietitian

How to Use *Meals For Good Health*
You will hear how others use the book to lose weight and be healthier. View the short videos.

Meals For Good Health Resources
You can order the *Meals for Good Health* CD or DVD or the *Sugar Check Kit.* The CD/DVD is a great compliment to the book. The book is also available in French.

Recipes
New recipes are being added regularly.

Newsletters
Karen's advice column is easy to read. I answer your health questions. You'll also find recipes and nutrition information tips.

Lifestyle Quiz
See how you rate. Take the Quiz now, then retake it in six months or one year.

Meal Portion Control
An easy guide showing how much to eat at your main meal, using your hands as portion guides.

Your Daily Calories
The online calorie counter (in metric or standard) will calculate how many calories you need to maintain your weight.

Your Nutrients
Find out about the different nutrients you need. The nutrients listed in the nutrient boxes in this book, are listed in this chart.

Links
Here are some links to other recommended nutrition and health websites.

Contact Us
If you have any questions or comments, you can contact me or the publisher.

So, let's get started.

It is difficult to lose weight, and I understand that well. If you use the tips, recipes, meals and snacks in Meals for Good Health, *you will lose weight slowly. You will feel better once you are eating healthy foods and exercising. If you lose one or two pounds a month, you will be doing great.*

Ideas for Healthy Living

Making Changes

Changing how you eat will take time. The biggest change will be eating less food. It is true that we become overweight because we eat too much food and we don't exercise enough.

During my counseling sessions, some people tell me they don't eat a lot of food. But if you eat the same amount of food as you did when you were ten years younger, and you have gained weight, then you are eating too much food. As you get older you need less food because your body slows down and you are not as active.

When you eat more food than your body needs, the extra food is changed into body fat. It does not matter whether that extra food is meat, bread, cookies or butter; the extra food becomes body fat.

Here are some tips to help you lose weight and gain health.

Eat breakfast

Do you eat breakfast? Many people say they are not hungry in the morning and they do not want the extra calories. They are not hungry in the morning because they eat a big dinner and snack too much in the evening. In the morning, they are still full from the night before.

When you eat breakfast, even a piece of fruit or a slice of toast, you have more energy. Your body will also "switch on" and start using up your fat. If you overeat in the evening, when you are less active, your body will store fat.

Let me suggest two changes. First, start eating a small breakfast. Second, eat less in the evening.

Drink water

Everyone needs to drink water. Water is good for you and it has no calories. It helps to fill your stomach. Drinking water is so important for losing weight that I have written a whole chapter about water.

Fill up on vegetables and fruit

These foods are naturally low in fat and are full of fiber, vitamins and minerals. If you eat more vegetables and fruit, you will find it easier to cut back on meats, fats, desserts and high-fat snack foods.

Divide your plate

Vegetables
1/2 of your plate; try to have two kinds of vegetables

Protein
1/4 of your plate; such as lean meat, chicken, fish, beans or lentils

Starch
1/4 of your plate; such as potatoes, rice, pasta or bread

Eat slowly

We have all eaten too quickly, then later said "I'm stuffed." Slow down and enjoy a smaller amount of food, for a little longer.

Save leftovers for the next meal

My grandmother used to say she got fat on shame because "it was a shame to see food go to waste."

Brush your teeth

Brush your teeth after a meal or snack. This may help keep you from feeling hungry so soon. I find this is a good way to stop overeating in the evening.

Go grocery shopping only after you've eaten

If I am hungry when I go grocery shopping, I am easily tempted to buy cakes and extra snacks. I try to go shopping after a meal. Then I can control myself and stay away from high-fat snacks and desserts. It works, try it.

Try making these small changes. These changes are a great way to start losing weight. Read on and you'll learn about some other changes that you can make when you are ready.

Limit restaurant meals

I suggest that you limit restaurant meals. Restaurant meals may seem to be a treat, but they are often high in fat and sugar. The month of meals in this book shows you just a few restaurant meals. These meals can also be made at home.

Weigh yourself no more than once a month

Your body weight goes up and down every day by one or two pounds, so it's not a good idea to weigh yourself every day. If you weigh yourself once a month, you will notice a gradual weight loss. If you lose one or two pounds a month you are doing well, because these pounds will stay off.

If you do not have a weigh scale, have your doctor, dietitian or health worker weigh you at least once a year.

If you are overweight by forty or fifty pounds or more, it probably took ten or more years to put that weight on. Expect to lose weight slowly. Losing ten pounds in one year would be a great success for anyone.

Go for a walk

Walking makes you feel better and helps you lose weight.

Eating Less Fat

One of the best things you can do for your heart and to lower your risk for some kinds of cancer, is to eat less fat, particularly saturated fat (animal fat) and trans fat. And, if you want to lose weight, you also need to eat less fat.

However, several kinds of fats, found in a variety of foods, are beneficial to your heart. To help you through the confusion about fats, I've grouped fats into three kinds: Unhealthy Fats, Healthy Fats and Healthiest Fats.

Unhealthy Fats

These fats need to be limited (but not totally avoided).
Saturated fat found in:
- lard, butter, and meat gravy
- meats such as beef, pork, lamb, chicken and turkey
- processed meats such as bacon, bologna, wieners, salami, sausages, liverwurst and canned meats
- eggs, high-fat hard cheese and cottage cheese, cream cheese, cream, high-fat sour cream and whole and partial-fat milk
- ice cream, chocolate, cookies, and baked goods
- deep fried foods and fast foods such as French fries, fried chicken, hamburgers and hot dogs
- coconut, coconut oil and palm oil

Cholesterol found in:
- most of the animal foods listed above
- liver and organ meats

Trans fats are man-made from vegetable oils, and found in:
- shortening and brick and hydrogenated margarine
- foods processed with hydrogenated and partially hydrogenated fat such as French fries, potato chips, microwave popcorn, peanut butter, crackers, cookies and baked goods such as donuts
- smaller amounts, occurring naturally, in animal foods including beef, bologna, butter and milk fats

Check food labels—
trans fats are called:
- "hydrogenated vegetable oil"
- "hydrogenated palm oil"
- or may be listed as "partially hydrogenated"
- "vegetable shortening"

Moderation and portion control is the best message for good health

In *Meals for Good Health,* meals that have higher amounts of saturated fat, trans fats or cholesterol are limited in portions and frequency so that your total fat intake is reasonable. For example, the meal plans encourage:
- small portions of meat or other protein
- low-fat dairy products such as skin milk
- small portions of desserts and snacks
- limited portions of spreads, regardless of whether you use margarine, butter or mayonaise

Ways to include polyunsaturated and monounsaturated fats in your meals and snacks:

- Avocado Salad—see "Newsletters" at **mealsforgoodhealth.com**

- Olives are included with Lunch 4 and Dinner 29. At just 7–10 calories per olives, they can be chosen as a Low-Calorie Snack.

- Seeds and nuts as a snack. As an alternative to meat, use almonds in the Dinner 27 Stir Fry or sunflower seeds in the Dinner 22 Sun Burgers.

- Fish-based lunches and dinners; for example Dinner 3, 5 and 23.

- Sardines on crackers, herring on pumpernickel bread or 12 half walnut pieces, or half an avocado. See Large Snacks section.

- Jumbo shrimp from the Medium Snacks section.

- Ground flaxseed: add 1–2 teaspoons (only 12 calories per teaspoon) daily to your oatmeal, pancake or muffin batter, or to cereal, salad, soup or stews.

- Purslane makes a nice addition to your green salad or soup.

Healthy Fats

Omega-6 polyunsaturated fat and monosaturated fats found in:

- vegetable oils such as canola, corn, olive, peanut, safflower, sunflower and flaxseed oil

- soft tub non-hydrogenated margarines or salad dressings, made from these oils

- avocados, olives and olive oil are rich in monounsaturated fats. These fats can help reduce blood cholesterol.

- nuts such as almonds, hazelnuts, pecans, peanuts, pistachios and walnuts

- seeds such as sunflower, sesame and flax seeds

Healthiest Fats

Omega-3 polyunsaturated fat is healthy for your brain and eyes. Research shows it may lower your risk for heart attacks and stroke because it lowers triglycerides (blood fat) and helps keep the blood from clotting.

Fish, especially cold water ocean fish, is the best source of omega-3 fats. Fish can also contain some omega-6 fat, monounsaturated fat or smaller amounts of saturated fat. Fish is rich in selenium, B vitamins and vitamin D. I recommend eating fish as part of a healthy diet. Due to pollution in fresh and salt water, if you are pregnant, check with your doctor before regularly including fish in your diet.

Omega-3 fat is found in:

- sardines, salmon, trout, bass, mackerel, herring, anchovies, sturgeon, halibut and tuna

- shellfish such as shrimp, lobster, clams, oysters, mussels and snow crab

- ground flaxseed or flaxseed oil; pumpkin seeds

- non-hydrogenated canola oil or soybean oil, or the margarines or salad dressings made from these oils

- walnuts

- eggs (in omega-3 enriched eggs, the chickens have generally been fed flax seed)

- soy nuts, soy beans, soy flour or wheat germ

- purslane, *Portulaca oleracea;* this plant is known as a garden "weed" yet is a source of omega-3 fat

Foods Rich in Monounsaturated Fats and Polyunsaturated Fats

Let's go on a grocery tour and look for hidden fat!

- Food labels list the amount of fat. Fat is listed in grams. Five grams (5 g) of fat is the same as 1 teaspoon of fat. On a box of crackers, serving sizes will vary. If one serving of three to five crackers has 5 g of fat, you will eat a whole teaspoon of fat when you eat those three crackers. That is a lot of hidden fat. A serving of three to five crackers with 2 g of fat or less would be a better choice.

- Foods labeled as *light* or *lite* may have less fat in them than the regular brands. Compare the labels of the light brand with the regular brand. Buy the one with the least amount of fat. For example, *light* hot chocolate has less fat and less sugar than regular hot chocolate. When a food is labeled as *light*, however, it may simply mean that the food is a light color. So check the label before you buy a food.

- *Low-fat* foods are usually good choices. These foods have less vegetable fat and less animal fat than the regular brands. One serving of a low-fat food must have less than about half a teaspoon of fat (3 g). Look for low-fat mayonnaise, low-fat margarine and low-fat cheese.

- *Calorie-reduced* foods are also good choices. They have fewer calories because they have less fat or sugar than the regular brand.

- One tablespoon of *fat-free* or *oil-free* salad dressing or *fat-free* sour cream has very little fat and very few calories. These are good choices.

- When a label says *cholesterol-free* the food will be low in cholesterol and animal fat (saturated fat) but it may still be loaded with vegetable fat, hydrogenated (trans) fat and calories. For example, frozen french fries labeled *cholesterol-free* are made with vegetable oil. Remember, animal fat and vegetable fat have the same high number of calories.

Check the label and choose foods that are:
- *light*
- *low-fat*
- *calorie-reduced*
- *fat-free*

A food that has fewer than 10 calories in a serving is so low in calories that it will not have an effect on your weight.

- Let's look at the amount of fat in milk, and talk about what kinds of milk are best for most adults. In whole milk, half the calories come from fat. This is not a good choice, as we do not need all this fat. By choosing 2 percent milk, you will get less fat than in whole milk. In 1 percent milk, one-quarter of the calories still come from fat, and this is a better choice than 2 percent milk. Skim milk is fat-free so it is the best choice for most adults. It may take time to get used to the new taste of skim milk, but it is a refreshing drink.

Note: On a label, % M.F. (percent milk fat) or % B.F. (percent butter fat) tells you how much fat is in a food, such as milk or cheese. Choose the one with the lowest percent fat.

- Look carefully at the luncheon meats, such as salami and bologna, and sausages and bacon. These meats have a lot of fat. Try to buy fewer of these and choose instead lean slices of ham, chicken, turkey or roast beef. A couple of the meals in this book do include a high-fat meat choice, such as wieners or sausages, but you'll see that because of the fat, the portions are small.

- Last on the tour, we check the amount of fat and sugar in cookies, cakes and snacks. There are many low-fat crackers, such as soda crackers, melba toast and rice cakes. You may also be able to find baked snack foods with no added fat, for example, baked corn chips. These are good choices.

I suggest you try to avoid the bakeshop and the chip and cookie aisles when you go shopping.

  All cookies and cakes have some fat and sugar. Arrowroot biscuits, social teas, digestive cookies and angel food cake are not as rich in fat as others.

  Some cookies or chocolate bars may be marked as *carbohydrate-reduced* or *sugar-free*. These may contain other sweeteners, such as sorbitol, and they often have a lot of fat added to them.

- Check the ingredients list on packaged foods. It is important to know that the first ingredients listed are the main ingredients. For example, if vegetable or palm oil is listed first, you will know the food is high in fat. If sugar, honey or glucose is listed first, this means the food is high in sugar.

More tips to help you eat less fat.

Add less fat to your food

Before you put butter, margarine, mayonnaise, cream or gravy on your food, ask yourself if you really need it. Try eating less of these fats. When you want a topping or spread, try a small amount of one of the low-fat or fat-free brands.

Take the fat off meat, chicken and fish

Trim the fat off meats, and take the skin off chicken, turkey or fish before cooking. Chicken or fish with the skin left on can have just as much fat as fatty red meats.

Low-fat baking tip:

Cut out at least half the fat called for in cake and muffin recipes. To keep your muffins or cake moist, add a small amount of skim milk yogurt or applesauce, as in the muffin recipe on page 64.

Cook foods without adding fat

Many foods can be cooked in fat-free ways. Foods can be boiled, steamed, broiled or barbecued. Try steamed fish, broiled sausages or chicken, or barbecued corn on the cob. If you occasionally want to fry foods, use a non-stick pan and don't add fat. Or cook in a heavy pan with some water or broth, or use a cooking spray, so the food doesn't stick to the pan.

Eat smaller portions of meat, chicken and fish

Now that you have cut off the extra fat and you are cooking without fat, you should try eating smaller portions of the meat, chicken and fish. Even if they are lean, they will still have hidden fat.

Try other flavorings on vegetables

Lightly cook your vegetables and they will be more tasty. Then sprinkle them with lemon juice or spices instead of butter or margarine. A sprinkle of dill, parsley, pepper or garlic can really make your vegetables taste good.

Put less fat on your sandwiches

Spread your sandwiches with a small amount of salsa, mustard, relish or light mayonnaise. Limit added fat.

Congratulations! You are now eating much less fat.

Do you use butter or margarine?

Many people tell me that they use only 100% vegetable oil or margarine, with no cholesterol or trans fat. I agree these are good choices.

But vegetable fats still have the same number of calories as butter or lard, which are animal fats. Fat is fattening, whether it's vegetable fat or animal fat. We need to eat less of all kinds of fats.

Many people believe bread and potatoes are fattening, so they cut down on these foods. But it is the fats we add to the bread and potatoes that is fattening. For example:
- the margarine we put on our bread
- the butter and sour cream we add to a baked potato
- or eating potatoes as potato chips and French fries

A healthier choice is to reduce the fat we add to food—try a small or medium potato as part of a balanced meal topped with just light sour cream and green onion tops for extra flavour.

Choose a variety of foods in the portions shows in *Meals for Good Health* and you will get the right amount of fats and other nutrients—avoid the temptation to add loads of butter or margarine to your foods.

All fats have the same calories—whether lard, butter, margarine or oil.

How much fat should you eat at each meal?

- The added fat should not be more than the tip of your thumb (1–2 teaspoons).

- This includes fat added during cooking as well as at the table.

Fish is the best source of omega-3 fat

Enjoy fish as part of a healthy diet.

Remember, the best diet for disease prevention
is eating less fat and exercising more.

You can get "healthy" fats in a healthy balanced diet
by following the ***Meals for Good Health*** meal plans.

Drinking More Water

Dietitians suggest drinking eight glasses of water a day. Eight glasses equals a two-liter plastic soft drink bottle. Many of us get much of our water in our coffee, tea, juice or soft drinks each day. But our bodies don't need all the caffeine or sugar in these drinks. Feel free to drink some coffee, tea or diet soft drinks, but also drink lots of plain water. It is the best calorie-free food.

It is a good habit to regularly drink water. Water helps keep you regular. Water helps reduce your thirst when you exercise.

Here are some tips to help you start drinking more water.

Drink 8 glasses of water each day.

Remind yourself

Often we simply forget to drink water. If you like water cold, keep a bottle or jug of water in the fridge. Keep a water glass on your table. When you see the jug or glass, you will remember to drink water.

Drink water in the morning

We are naturally thirsty when we first wake up. Drink water first thing in the morning.

Drink water with meals

Get into the habit of having one glass of water or more with all your meals and snacks. Add a slice of lemon to your water for a fresh taste.

Drink water whenever you feel hungry

Water fills your stomach so you feel full and eat less.

Water makes life flow. Go with the flow.

Eating More Starches

Grains and starches are the staple foods for most people around the world. They include grains, such as wheat and oats, corn, rice, potatoes, lentils, beans and cassava. Grains and starches are made into breakfast cereals and are ground into flour to make breads, pitas, tortillas, noodles, bannocks and rotis.

Starches provide energy, are low in fat and are low in cost. They are bulk foods that help us feel full. Starches add vitamins and minerals to our diet. The energy we obtain from starch is the preferred source of energy for our brain, muscles and nerves.

Fiber is another important part of many starch foods, such as whole wheat or rye breads. Fiber is a natural laxative. Much of the fiber has been taken out of white flour.

The North American diet has changed over the last century. We now eat fewer starch foods and we eat more meat and processed foods. Processed foods have added fat, sugar and salt. So we are eating more fat. We suffer from diseases that are linked to eating too much fat, such as diabetes, heart disease and cancer.

Losing weight means eating less fat. That means eating less meat and less added fat. Then starches and vegetables can start filling up more of your plate.

You will find that all the meals in *Meals for Good Health* include grains or starches, with little or no added fat.

Grains and other starches:
- *give you energy*
- *are low in fat*
- *help you feel full*
- *have fiber*
- *have vitamins and minerals*

How much starch should you eat at your meals?
- Have a starch food with every meal.
- Size of your fist for your main meal.

Grains and Starches

Filling Up on Vegetables & Fruits

Avocado and olives are two fruits that have little natural sugar but a lot of monosaturated fat.

Eating vegetables and fruits gives you energy. They are low in fat. Like starch foods, they add vitamins, minerals and extra fiber to your diet. They help reduce your risk for cancer.

Fresh or frozen vegetables and fruits are the best. Check the label and choose frozen ones that do not have salt, fat or sugar added.

Fruit canned in water or juice is a better choice than fruit canned in syrup. Drain off most of the juice. Canned vegetables usually have salt, and sometimes sugar, added. Choose these less often.

You may be surprised to learn that "unsweetened" fruit juices have sugar. One cup of unsweetened apple, orange or grapefruit juice has 6 to 7 teaspoons of natural sugar. Grape and prune juice have almost 10 teaspoons of sugar in a cup. Since juice has less fiber and is not as filling as fresh fruit, it is easy to drink too much. If you drink a lot of juice, it will be hard for you to lose weight.

Vegetable juices, such as tomato juice, have less sugar than fruit juices. For this reason, several meals shown include a small glassful. When you are thirsty, drink water, not juices.

Dried fruit has more sugar than fresh fruit because the water has been taken out. For example, 2 tablespoons of raisins has 4 teaspoons of sugar; about the same amount of sugar as 1/2 cup of grapes.

Many of the lunches and dinners shown have two or more vegetables. This may be more than you are used to eating. It is an important change. Most of the breakfasts include fruit. Fruit is often the dessert for lunch or dinner.

When you are hungry between meals, eating a vegetable or a fruit would be better than eating a high-fat snack food or a rich dessert. Low-fat starch foods are also good for snacks. You will find a variety of snack choices on pages 222-229.

How many vegetables and fruits should you eat?

- Include a fruit with breakfast.
- Include two or more vegetables at lunch and dinner, and a fruit if you'd like.
- Choose a fruit or vegetable for a snack.
- Hold your two hands together and overfill them with vegetables and fruits and you will have a good daily amount.

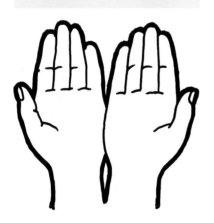

Vegetables & Fruits

Choosing Milk & Calcium-Rich Foods

Calcium is found in milk and foods made from milk.

Calcium is a mineral that makes your bones and teeth strong. It is found in milk and foods made from milk, such as yogurt and cheese. Calcium is also found in other foods, such as dried beans and a few other vegetables and soft fish bones.

Calcium is important for adults as well as for children.

Infants and growing children need lots of calcium as their bones and teeth grow. Many people believe that milk and other calcium foods are just for kids. The truth is, we need calcium all our adult life to keep our bones strong.

Does drinking milk give you stomach pains? If so, you may not be able to fully digest the natural sugar (lactose) in the milk. You may be able to digest just small amounts of milk and foods made from milk, such as cheese or yogurt. You could also drink lactose-reduced skim milk.

You can get your daily calcium from other foods, such as:
- tofu made with added calcium
- soy or rice drinks and fruit juice made with added calcium
- beans, such as baked beans
- seeds and nuts, such as almonds and sesame seeds
- fish bones, such as those in canned salmon
- dark green, leafy vegetables, such as broccoli, Brussels sprouts, okra, kale and Chinese cabbage
- a few fruits, such as dried figs and oranges

How much milk and calcium-rich food should you eat?
- At every meal, try to include 1–2 servings of low-fat calcium-rich foods.
- For a serving, have a half to one cup of milk or yogurt, a bowlful of a vegetable like cabbage, or a thumb-size amount of a solid food like cheese, nuts or tofu.

Choose low-fat, calcium-rich foods, such as:
- low-fat milk, low-fat yogurt (skim or 1 percent) and low-fat cheeses (less than 20 percent milk fat)
- skim milk powder
- salmon canned in water, not oil
- low-fat soy milk (some have extra sugar added)
- dark green, leafy vegetables and beans are naturally low in fat

Seeds, nuts and tofu have vegetable fat; they can be chosen in the amounts shown in the meals.

Most of the meals in *Meals for Good Health* include one or more calcium-rich foods. Add an extra daily serving to meet the new increased daily recommendations.

cheese

milk

Calcium-Rich Foods

Eating the Right Amount of Protein

You need only a small amount of protein each day.

Proteins are important to keep you healthy. However, we only need a small amount of protein every day. The meals in this book show you how much protein to eat.

You can easily get protein from animal foods, such as meat, eggs and milk. Proteins are also found in nuts, seeds, and many vegetables and grains. I have included a variety of vegetable and animal proteins in the meals.

Vegetable proteins

Kidney beans, brown beans, chickpeas and dried peas are low-fat vegetable proteins. Tofu is made from soy beans and can replace meat. Smaller amounts of vegetable protein are found in starch foods, such as whole wheat bread and oatmeal.

Nuts, including peanuts or peanut butter, and seeds, such as sunflower seeds, are high-fat vegetable proteins. They can still be a good choice for some meals, in the right amounts.

How much protein should you eat?
- Size of the palm of your hand for your main meal.
- For women, this usually means about 3–5 ounces of cooked meat or other protein, and for men, about 4–7 ounces.

Animal proteins

Lean red meats are a good choice for low-fat animal protein. They include lean hamburger, and fat-trimmed round roast or steak, loin lamb or pork chop, and deer or rabbit. Chicken and turkey are a good source of protein, but remember to remove the skin.

Eggs are a good source of protein. Do you ask, "Can I eat eggs with high blood cholesterol?" Yes, you can safely eat three eggs a week. There are other important ways to reduce your high blood cholesterol (see page 45).

Choose fish as part of a healthy diet.

Most fish with the skin taken off has less fat than red meat. Some of the best low-fat fish are pike, pickerel, ocean perch, red snapper, cod, haddock and sole. Tuna, pink salmon and sardines canned in water are good choices too. Shrimp and lobster are also low in fat. Blue fish is a medium-fat fish. The fattier fishes are lake trout or red (sockeye) salmon; eat smaller portions of these. Try to eat fish at least once a week.

Meats and Other Proteins

Choosing Fiber

Fiber is in:
- *starch foods*
- *vegetables*
- *fruits*

You *can be regular without using laxatives.*

Here *are a* **FEW** *steps to prevent constipation:*
- **Fiber**
- **Exercise**
- **Water**

More *fiber information and recipes at* **mealsforgoodhealth.com** *link to "Newsletters" and "Recipes".*

The natural way to be regular is to eat high-fiber foods, drink lots of water and exercise. Fiber is also important if you have diabetes or heart disease, and for reducing your risk for certain kinds of cancer.

One question I ask my clients is whether they are often constipated. It is a personal question, but it can tell me what they eat. Being regular depends so much on what you eat. People who eat many high-fiber starch foods, vegetables and fruits do not usually become constipated.

If you are sometimes constipated, you should know that you can be regular without laxatives. If you have been taking laxatives often or for a long time, this may have caused you to have a lazy bowel.

Start eating more high-fiber foods. Add these high-fiber foods to your diet slowly so that you won't get cramps and gas. Drink lots of water. Go for walks. Your bowel muscles will get stronger and start to work for you again. As you make these changes over the next few months, you may not need a laxative at all.

By combining daily meals and snacks from *Meals for Good Health,* you will get the amount of fiber recommended for most adults (20–35 grams per day), or more. To offer variety, some lower fiber choices are included in *Meals for Good Health,* such as white bread, but these are complemented with high fiber choices at the same meal. You will find a good balance between soluble fiber (found in oat bran, bean and legumes and some fruits) and insoluble fiber (found in wheat bran, and fruits and vegetables). Soluble fiber helps reduce the rate at which sugars are absorbed into the blood stream. Insoluble fiber acts as a bulking agent and helps reduce constipation and may help prevent certain bowel diseases. Both forms of fiber are helpful if you are trying to lose weight, as they make your meals bulkier and help you to feel full.

Eat More Fiber Foods

Getting All Your Vitamins & Minerals

Spend your money on healthy foods instead of vitamin and mineral pills.

Vitamins and minerals are found in all foods. Extra vitamins and minerals have been added to many foods, such as breads, cereals and milk. By eating a variety of healthy foods, as shown in this book, you will get the vitamins and minerals that your body needs. These foods will help keep you healthy and reduce your chance of becoming ill.

You only need tiny amounts of vitamins and minerals to keep you healthy. For example, you need 70-90 milligrams of Vitamin C every day; which is found in one large orange. If you also take a pill of 1000 milligrams (or 1 gram) of Vitamin C every day, your kidneys have to work harder to flush out the extra Vitamin C.

Some foods, such as soda pop and coffee, are low in vitamins and minerals — limit these poor food choices.

Your healthy body looks after you, storing the vitamins and minerals that you need for later. For example, Vitamin A is stored mostly in your liver, and iron is stored in your liver, bone marrow, spleen and muscles. If you take these vitamins or minerals as pills, your body may end up with more than you need.

You do not need to take vitamin and mineral pills unless your doctor or dietitian has prescribed them. If a vitamin or mineral pill is prescribed for you, be sure to ask why, and know how many you should take.

Nutrient tables and menu boxes
For each meal and recipe, you will find a table listing nutrition information.

*Would you like to find out how much vitamin C, calcium, iron or other nutrients you need? Visit **mealsforgoodhealth.com***

Limiting Sugar, Salt & Alcohol

Limiting sugar

Sugar is found naturally in fruits, vegetables and even milk. Starches found in breads and cereals break into sugar after you eat them. The sugar in these foods gives you energy. These foods also have many other nutrients. These foods are good for you in the amounts shown in the meals and snacks.

We need to limit pure sugars—white sugar, brown sugar, icing sugar, corn syrup, maple syrup, molasses and honey. One type of pure sugar is not better or worse than another. These pure sugars give us calories we don't need and very little nutrition. Such sugars are called "empty calories."

Sugars are added to most of our processed foods. In fact, it is hard to find a food label without sugar on the ingredient list. If sugar is the first ingredient, it means the food has more sugar than anything else. Try to limit foods that have a lot of added sugar.

Lots of sugar can be found in what you drink. High-sugar drinks include chocolate milk, milk shakes, fruit drinks, fruit crystal drinks, fruit juice and regular soft drinks. One cup of unsweetened fruit juice or 1 cup of regular soft drink has about 7 teaspoons of sugar. Choose water or diet drinks instead.

You may see words such as sucrose, fructose, sorbitol and mannitol on food labels. Sucrose and fructose are pure sugars and they are not low-calorie. Sorbitol and mannitol are types of sugars that have slightly fewer calories than table sugar and they raise the blood sugar more slowly.

Look out for cookies, candies and chocolates made with sorbitol, they are often high in fat. These foods are not low-calorie. In fact, they may have similar calories to the regular cookies, candies or chocolates. Limit all of them.

Different cereals have different amounts of sugar:

Bran Flakes – have a small amount of sugar added (1 teaspoon or 4 grams in 3/4 cup).

Frosted Flakes – have a large amount of sugar added (3 teaspoons or 12 grams in 3/4 cup).

*Sucrose, fructose, sorbitol and mannitol are **not** low-calorie sweeteners.*

*Equal, Splenda, Sugar Twin, Sweet N' Low and Steevia **are** low-calorie sweeteners.*

Low-sugar baking tip:

When making your favorite recipe for muffins, cookies or cakes, cut the sugar in half. This reduced amount of sugar will still be enough for them to rise nicely. If you feel that your recipe is not sweet enough, you can add some low-calorie sweetener, such as Splenda or Sugar Twin.

Sweeteners that have Nutrasweet, such as Equal, shouldn't be used for baking; they lose their sweetness when cooked.

Low-calorie sweeteners

Instead of sugar you may want to try using low-calorie sweeteners in your coffee, tea or on your cereal. Some common brand names are Equal (Nutrasweet), Splenda, Sugar Twin, Sweet N' Low and Steevia. Low-calorie sweeteners have a lot less sugar and fewer calories than real sugar. Because these sweeteners have few calories, three or four packages (or teaspoons) a day would have little effect on your weight or blood sugar level. Foods that have low-calorie sweeteners added include diet soft drinks, light puddings, light gelatin and sugar-free gum.

One teaspoon of sugar has the same sweetness as 1 teaspoon of Splenda or 1/2 teaspoon of Sugar Twin or Sweet N'Low. If you find these sweeteners "super sweet," use a little less.

Added sugar in recipes and meals

In a few *Meals for Good Health* dessert recipes sugar is used instead of fat. Sugar has fewer calories than fat. In the same way, small amounts of jam or syrup are included in some breakfasts, in place of margarine. This amount of sugar is part of a healthy diet, even if you have diabetes (see pages 45-47 to learn more about diabetes).

When you start choosing low-fat foods and eating fewer processed foods, you will be eating less fat and sugar.

You are on your way to losing weight.

Limiting salt

Salt gives us sodium, an important mineral. Sodium occurs naturally in foods. You need only a small amount of sodium for good health.

Iodized salt provides us with iodine. Iodine is essential to keep your thyroid healthy. The thyroid regulates how you burn calories. A small amount of iodized salt gives you all the iodine you need. Seafood is also an excellent source of iodine—another reason to eat fish at least once or twice a week.

Unfortunately, most of us get more salt than we need. We eat too many salty processed foods and many of us add too much salt to our food. This extra salt in our diet makes extra work for our kidneys.

Cutting back on salt is a good healthy change for everyone. If you have high blood pressure, cutting back on salt may help reduce your blood pressure. However, for some people with high blood pressure, making other changes including losing weight, exercising and quitting smoking may be more helpful (see page 45).

Cutting back on salt means shaking a little less salt on your food, adding less salt (or no salt) to your recipes and limiting salty foods.

Try these tips to cut back on salt:
- Season your food during cooking and at the table with spices and herbs, lemon juice, lime juice or vinegar.
- Use lots of pepper instead of salt.
- Use garlic powder or onion powder instead of garlic salt or onion salt.
- Use less salt in cooking and baking. For many recipes you don't need to add any salt.
- Look for low-sodium or unsalted foods, such as unsalted soda crackers.
- Choose fresh or frozen vegetables instead of canned.
- Eat less take-out and restaurant meals. They are high in salt and fat.

Salt is added to most processed foods.

Once you start to cut back on salt, you will notice that many foods begin to taste too salty.

Salt in *Meals for Good Health* recipes:

- Salt is not added to the recipes unless needed for rising or recipe quality.
- The flavor of some of the recipes is enhanced by the salt found in the dried bouillon powder, dried soup mix or soy sauce. Use less of these if you need to cut out more salt, and instead use more spices and herbs. You can also buy reduced-salt bouillon powder, low-salt soups, and light soy sauce.

Salt in *Meals for Good Health* meals:

- The meals in this book will help you cut back on salt.
- Some salty foods, such as dill pickles, sauerkraut, sausages, ham and wieners are part of the meals. In the portions shown, these can be part of a healthy diet.
- If you need to cut out more of your salt, then you could choose:
  - sliced cucumber instead of a dill pickle
  - plain cabbage instead of sauerkraut
  - unsalted beef or pork instead of sausages or wieners
  - leftover cooked meat or chicken, or an egg instead of processed meat on sandwiches

Limiting alcohol

If you want to lose weight, you must look at everything you eat and drink, including alcohol. **Alcohol is high in calories.** Like sugar, alcohol is full of "empty calories." In this book you will find a glass of wine as an option with one of the meals. A light beer and shot of whiskey are shown in the snack photographs as occasional choices only. **Daily intake of alcohol should be only on the advice of your doctor.**

The calories in hard liquor, such as whiskey, come from the alcohol alone. Three-quarters of the calories in beer comes from the alcohol with the rest coming mostly from sugar. In liqueurs, just over half the calories come from alcohol and the rest come from sugar.

One beer or two ounces of hard liquor, such as whiskey or rum, have about the same number of calories as two slices of bread.

Six beers have 900 calories. That's a lot. Six diet soft drinks have only 20 calories.

To reduce calories from alcoholic drinks:

- Drink less beer, wine, liqueurs and hard liquor. Instead drink water, diet beverages, no-alcohol low-calorie beer, or coffee or tea.
- Choose a light or extra light beer, which has less sugar and less alcohol than regular beer.
- Instead of drinking a whole beer, have just half a beer and mix it with diet ginger ale.
- Most of the no-alcohol beers and no-alcohol wines have sugar (though usually less sugar than soft drinks) but are still a better choice than beer that has alcohol.
- If you want to have a glass of wine, choose dry wine. This has less sugar than sweet wine.
- Avoid liqueurs, which are heavy on alcohol and sugar.
- If you choose to have a drink of hard liquor, mix it with a diet soft drink or water instead of juice or regular soft drinks.
- Drink water before and with your meals, instead of alcohol. Alcohol often makes you feel hungrier.

Alcohol is more than just a source of calories, it is an addictive drug. If you drink a lot of alcohol, it will be affecting more than your weight. Alcohol will make it hard to make other changes in your life.

Drinking less alcohol is a difficult choice but it's okay to ask for help.

Think about making a change.

Caution:
- *Alcohol does not mix well with some pills– check the pill bottle label to see if it is okay to drink alcohol.*
- *If you have diabetes and take insulin or diabetes pills, drinking alcohol can cause a low blood sugar reaction. To avoid this problem, limit your drinks to one or two; and have something to eat with your drink.*
- *Alcohol is not recommended for children and teenagers, and women who are pregnant or breastfeeding.*

Walking for Health

To lose weight, you need regular exercise.

Walking is the best exercise for most of us.

Three important things you will learn from this book are to eat less food, eat less fat and exercise more. It is a dream to think you can lose weight without regular exercise.

Walking is one of the best kinds of exercise. You can walk when you want and where you want. Start off slowly and try walking a little faster and further each week.

Most of the people I counsel say they are active. I tell them that there is a difference between being active (or busy) and exercising. I compare the way we live today with the lives of our grandparents. People used to walk to work, to the store, to the post office, to school, to church and to the dance hall. Working in the home and on the farm was a lot of hard exercise. Today, we don't walk enough. We sit or stand for hours a day, whether at home or at work. Television and computers too often replace active play and work. This lack of exercise makes us unhealthy.

You will find that exercise gives you more energy.

Are you simply too tired to go for a walk? When your muscles are weak, you will feel tired. If you are overweight, going for a walk may even hurt. It may seem strange, but the only way to have the energy for walking is to go for a walk. Once you become more fit, you will find that walking gives you energy.

Are you so busy you can't find the time to go for a walk? Finding the time for a walk means making a few changes. Think about how often you go outside to do something—such as start the car or go to the bus stop, or get the mail. Once you are outside, take an extra twenty minutes to go for a walk. Walking is an important part of keeping healthy. We usually can find the time to do things which we think are important.

Walking helps you lose weight and helps you in many other ways.

Walking can help you lose weight. It can also help you look and feel better. Walking keeps your bones and muscles strong. You will breathe deeper and easier. Walking often reduces back pain and other joint pain. Walking can help you reduce your stress and help you sleep better at night.

If you have diabetes, walking helps you lower your blood sugar. If you have high blood cholesterol, walking helps you lower your blood cholesterol. If you have high blood pressure, walking will help bring it down.

When I see a client two months after they have started walking, they tell me they feel healthier. They have often lost weight. They are now ready to do more walking, as it gets easier with each passing day.

It may take many months to get into a pattern of regular walking. Once you start walking more, you will feel better about yourself.

Put this book down and go for a walk.

Here are some helpful walking tips

First, start walking more each day.

When you go shopping, park at the far end of the lot and walk. When you take the bus, get off one stop early and walk that extra block.

Walking up and down stairs is great exercise. Start by walking down stairs.

Comfortable shoes or boots that fit well are important.

Then, start walking as a regular exercise.

Try to go for a walk twice a week. It may help to walk at the same time each day so it becomes a habit—a good habit. Your dog would love to go for a walk any time. Watching TV wastes a lot of good walking time.

Mark your calendar each day you go for a walk.

Boldly mark your calendar after each walk, and feel proud of yourself.

Next, walk further. Walk more often. Walk faster and swing your arms.

Walk faster and you will lose more weight.

You may also want to swim, bike or do other exercises.

Now that you are walking, you may decide to also do some swimming, biking or dancing. Using an exercise bike or a treadmill are also excellent ways to exercise. Good for you, if you start getting involved in other sports and activities.

Walking takes time, but it gives you a lifetime of better health. Enjoy!

Advice for Those with Diabetes or Heart Disease

The meal plans in *Meals for Good Health* will help you if you have diabetes. If you have heart disease, including high blood cholesterol, high triglycerides (blood fat) or high blood pressure, the meal plans are also suitable for you.

The advice for those of you with diabetes and heart disease is much the same as for everyone:
- lose weight if you are overweight
- eat a diet lower in fat, salt, sugar and alcohol
- eat a diet higher in starches, vegetables, fruit and fiber
- do not smoke
- exercise
- learn to relax
- take your pills and/or insulin as advised by your doctor
- have regular medical check-ups

If you have heart disease:

If you have high blood pressure, a doctor or dietitian may advise you to limit salt. As a dietitian, I know that it is not just salt that raises blood pressure. To lower blood pressure, it is also important to make the other changes listed above. These changes are also important for lowering blood cholesterol.

High triglycerides (blood fat) are often caused by high blood sugar. This is because some of the extra sugar in your blood is changed into blood fat. Another possible cause of high triglycerides is drinking too much alcohol—alcohol can also be changed into blood fat. If your triglycerides are high, you should take steps to bring down your blood sugar and to cut back or stop drinking alcohol.

If you have diabetes:

Eating less fat is important when you have diabetes or heart disease.

If you have diabetes, eating too much fat may be more of a problem than eating too much sugar. If you are overweight and you lose body fat, this will make your insulin work better and your blood sugar will improve. Walking and other exercise will also make your insulin work better and will bring down blood sugar levels.

As a person with diabetes, you are more likely to have heart problems. If you eat less fat and walk, this will be better for your heart. The advice for heart disease and diabetes are much the same—eat less fat, lose weight and exercise more.

It is also important to eat regular small meals, as shown in this book, rather than just one large meal a day. This helps to even out your food and sugar over the day, so you can control your blood sugar better.

Small amounts of sugar can safely be eaten by a person with diabetes.

It is now known that if you have diabetes, you can safely eat small amounts of sugar in the form of table sugar or candy. Of course, if you eat a large amount of a sweet food, you will have a quick and large rise in your blood sugar.

Are you carbohydrate counting?

The total amount of carbohydrate in the meals can vary up to about 2 slices of bread. Refer to the grams of carbohydrates listed for each meal, recipe, and snack. Talk to a dietitian for help with carbohydrate counting and insulin adjustment.

The meal plans in *Meals for Good Health* can safely be followed, even if you are taking insulin or diabetes pills. This is because the amount of carbohydrate (starch and sugar) in each meal is reasonable. There is some variation in the carbohydrate content of the meals and snacks, although the calories are the same. The carbohydrates are listed for each meal, recipe and snack.

You will find additional nutrient information about the meals, recipes and snacks shown in this book at **mealsforgoodhealth.com**

Read this if you are on diabetes pills, insulin, heart pills or blood pressure pills

- When you make changes, such as eating less or exercising more, you may not need as many pills or as much insulin. If you feel weak, shaky or dizzy when exercising, before meals or when getting out of bed, your pills may be too strong for you. See your doctor if you are not feeling well. Do not change your pills or insulin without talking to your doctor first.

- Ask your doctor or the pharmacist about what may happen if you drink alcohol when you are taking insulin, diabetes pills or heart pills.

If you are lean and do not need to lose weight

If you do not need to lose weight, you may wonder if you can still use this book. The answer is yes! Many changes that help a person lose weight, such as eating less fat and eating more fiber, are healthy changes for all of us. We all need different amounts of food. The "How to Use this Book" section on pages 5–11 will help you choose the right size meals and snacks.

You are doing great. Making changes takes time and effort—but you are worth it!

Meals, Recipes and Snacks

Breakfast Meals

- **each large breakfast has 370 calories**
- **each small breakfast has 250 calories**

BREAKFAST 1

Dry Cereal

Nutrition information for this meal is found in the table that you see below.

Please look for the tables on every meal page.

*To find out your nutrient needs, visit **mealsforgoodhealth.com***

This is the easiest breakfast to prepare.

Look at the cereal labels before you buy. Choose cereals that have little or no added sugar. One serving should have less than 5 grams of sugar and less than 2 grams of fat.

If a cereal is made with added dried fruit, such as raisins, it will have a higher amount of sugar. For example, 1 tablespoon of raisins adds an extra 5 grams of sugar. If you are choosing a cereal with added fruit, you should have a smaller portion of fruit on the side.

Another thing to look for when you buy cereals is fiber. Cereals with a lot of fiber are a good choice. These would include bran cereals and whole wheat cereals.

Skim milk and 1 percent milk have very little fat, and are the best choice for your cereal and for drinking. If you use canned milk, buy skim evaporated milk. Remember, 1/4 cup evaporated milk mixed with 1/4 cup water is the same as 1/2 cup regular milk.

Add fruit to your cereal or eat it on the side. Choose a half a banana or any of the fruits you see with the other breakfast meals. A 1/2 cup of unsweetened juice has the same calories as one small fruit, but it does not have the fiber.

	Per Large Meal	Per Small Meal
Carbohydrates	82 g	55 g
Protein	15.6 g	8.8 g
Fat	1.5 g	1.0 g
Saturated Fat	0.6 g	0.3 g
Cholesterol	4 mg	2 mg
Fiber	10.7 g	7.0 g
Sodium	676 mg	393 mg
Vitamin A	152 µg	77 µg
Folic Acid	65 µg	44 µg
Vitamin C	10 mg	9 mg
Potassium	1058 mg	720 mg
Calcium	336 mg	172 mg
Iron	8.6 mg	5.2 mg

Drink water with all your meals, including breakfast. If you have a cup of coffee or tea, go easy on the sugar. Cut it out if you can, or use a low-calorie sweetener. Also, go easy on the cream and coffee whitener. You probably know that cream has a lot of fat, but did you know that coffee whitener is made mostly with sugar and oil? Instead of using cream or coffee whitener, try using skim milk or skim milk powder. If you want to use coffee whitener, buy the light kind and limit yourself to a couple of teaspoons a day.

Your Breakfast Menu	Large Meal (370 calories)	Small Meal (250 calories)
Bran flakes cereal	1 1/4 cup	3/4 cup
Skim or 1 percent milk	1 cup	1/2 cup
Half a small banana	3-inch piece	3-inch piece

SMALL MEAL

BREAKFAST 2

Egg & Toast

Sugar, honey or jam have fewer calories than butter or margarine. This is because a gram of sugar has fewer calories than a gram of fat.
- *1 teaspoon of sugar, honey or regular jam or jelly has 20 calories.*
- *1 teaspoon of butter or margarine has about 40 calories.*

For your toast, choose brown bread, such as whole wheat or rye bread. These breads have a lot of fiber.

For a light choice, put a small amount of jam or honey on your toast, without butter or margarine.

Boil an egg, or poach or fry it in a non-stick pan with no added fat. Choose eggs that have been enriched with omega-3 fats to boost your heart health.

Large eggs have almost the same yolk size as small eggs. Large eggs are larger because they have more egg white. This means that a small egg has about the same cholesterol as a large egg.

A small serving of fruit or several slices of tomato goes with this meal. For a change, try 1/2 cup of tomato or vegetable juice. Tomato juice would be a light choice since it has half the sugar of fruit juice.

A note about fruit juice:
Fresh fruit is a better choice than fruit juice. This is because fresh fruit has more fiber and is more filling. However, you can choose 1/2 cup of unsweetened orange juice instead of one small orange.

Drink 1/2 cup of skim milk or 1 percent milk with this meal. One 1/2 cup of buttermilk is also low in fat.

	Per Large Meal	Per Small Meal
Carbohydrates	48 g	34 g
Protein	16.3 g	13.6 g
Fat	14.1 g	7.5 g
Saturated Fat	3.4 g	2.2 g
Cholesterol	218 mg	219 mg
Fiber	6.7 g	4.0 g
Sodium	529 mg	298 mg
Vitamin A	273 µg	200 µg
Folic Acid	71 µg	64 µg
Vitamin C	36 mg	36 mg
Potassium	538 mg	575 mg
Calcium	253 mg	227 mg
Iron	2.6 mg	1.8 mg

Your Breakfast Menu	Large Meal (370 calories)	Small Meal (250 calories)
Egg (cooked without fat)	1	1
Brown toast	2 slices	1 slice
Margarine	2 teaspoons	1/2 teaspoon
Jam or jelly	1 teaspoon	1 teaspoon
Skim or 1 percent milk	1/2 cup	1/2 cup
Orange slices	1/2 a 3-inch orange	1/2 a 3-inch orange

SMALL MEAL

Pancakes & Bacon

Look at the labels on light syrup. Two tablespoons should have fewer than 60 calories. Two tablespoons of this light syrup are the same as 1 tablespoon of most regular syrups.

For extra fiber, add 1 tablespoon of bran to your batter.

If you don't have a non-stick pan, coat your frying pan lightly with a greased paper towel, or use a cooking spray.

These thin pancakes are easy to make. They are lower in fat and sugar than the store-bought pancake mixes.

Syrup replaces fruit in this breakfast.

Cook your bacon until crisp. Reduce the fat by draining off the grease. One thin slice of lean ham or back bacon has less fat than the side of bacon shown. Because bacon is higher in saturated fat, choose it no more than once a week.

Low-Fat Pancakes

Makes sixteen 4-inch pancakes.

Each pancake
Calories: 68
Carbohydrate: 11 g
Protein: 2.7 g
Fat: 1.2 g

1 1/2 cups flour

1/2 teaspoon salt

1 teaspoon baking powder

1 tablespoon sugar

1 egg

1 tablespoon of oil, margarine or butter, melted

1 3/4 cups skim milk

1. In a large bowl mix together the flour, salt, baking powder and sugar.
2. In a medium bowl, beat the egg with a fork. Add the fat and milk to the egg, and mix well.
3. Add the egg mixture to the flour mixture. Stir until smooth. It helps to stir with a wire wisk. If it is too thick add a little more milk.
4. Cook on a non-stick pan, on medium heat or in an electric non-stick pan. Use just under 1/4 cup of batter for each pancake. Once the pancakes have small bubbles, turn them over.

	Per Large Meal	Per Small Meal
Carbohydrates	57 g	39 g
Protein	12.0 g	8.0 g
Fat	9.9 g	6.8 g
Saturated Fat	3.2 g	2.2 g
Cholesterol	53 mg	36 mg
Fiber	1.2 g	0.8 g
Sodium	525 mg	356 mg
Vitamin A	85 µg	57 µg
Folic Acid	14 µg	10 µg
Vitamin C	1 mg	0 mg
Potassium	244 mg	164 mg
Calcium	158 mg	105 mg
Iron	3.0 mg	2.0 mg

Your Breakfast Menu	Large Meal (370 calories)	Small Meal (250 calories)
Low-Fat Pancakes	3	2
Syrup	1 1/2 tablespoons, or 3 tablespoons of light syrup	1 tablespoon, or 2 tablespoons of light syrup
Bacon, crisp	2 strips	1 1/2 strips

SMALL MEAL

BREAKFAST 4

Toast & Peanut Butter

A light (or "diet") jam or jelly should have fewer than 10 calories in 1 teaspoon (30 calories in 1 tablespoon). 2 teaspoons of this light jam are about the same as 1 teaspoon of regular jam or jelly.

Jams marked "no sugar added" may in fact have added sugar in the form of concentrated fruit juice. These jams often have almost the same amount of sugar as regular jam.

This simple breakfast has protein to start your day. One tablespoon of peanut butter is a good source of protein. But peanut butter has a lot of fat, so put it on a dry piece of toast—you don't need to add extra fat.

Half an apple is served with this breakfast.

Here are a few examples of other fruit servings:
- a half cup of unsweetened applesauce
- one large kiwi
- a quarter of a small melon
- a half a small banana
- one orange
- a half a grapefruit. See Breakfast 8 for a new way to enjoy grapefruit.

In place of the 1/2 cup of milk, you may have 1 cup of light hot cocoa (see Breakfast 9).

For the large meal, try the peanut butter on your first piece of toast and 1 teaspoon of jam or jelly on your lightly buttered second piece of toast.

	Per Large Meal	Per Small Meal
Carbohydrates	53 g	34 g
Protein	13.5 g	10.9 g
Fat	13.7 g	9.2 g
Saturated Fat	2.7 g	1.8 g
Cholesterol	3 mg	3 mg
Fiber	7.7 g	4.9 g
Sodium	493 mg	291 mg
Vitamin A	124 µg	76 µg
Folic Acid	48 µg	34 µg
Vitamin C	5 mg	5 mg
Potassium	553 mg	472 mg
Calcium	211 mg	185 mg
Iron	2.2 mg	1.3 mg

Your Breakfast Menu	Large Meal (370 calories)	Small Meal (250 calories)
Brown toast	2 slices	1 slice
Peanut butter	1 tablespoon	1 tablespoon
Margarine or butter	1 teaspoon	–
Jam or jelly	1 teaspoon, or 2 teaspoons diet jam	– –
Skim or 1 percent milk	1/2 cup	1/2 cup
Apple slices	1/2 a 3-inch apple	1/2 a 3-inch apple

SMALL MEAL

BREAKFAST 5

Hot Cereal

Have a full fruit serving of fruit if you don't choose sugar:
- *2 tablespoons of raisins*
- *2 prunes or dried apricots*
- *1/4 cup prune juice.*

	Per Large Meal	Per Small Meal
Carbohydrates	**68 g**	**48 g**
Protein	**15.9 g**	**10.6 g**
Fat	**3.9 g**	**2.5 g**
Saturated Fat	0.8 g	0.5 g
Cholesterol	3 mg	2 mg
Fiber	6.2 g	4.2 g
Sodium	105 mg	70 mg
Vitamin A	112 µg	75 µg
Folic Acid	24 µg	16 µg
Vitamin C	2 mg	2 mg
Potassium	649 mg	445 mg
Calcium	271 mg	183 mg
Iron	3.0 mg	2.1 mg

Hot cereals such as porridge (oatmeal), oat bran, whole grain cereals and corn meal cereal are high in fiber. Adding 1 tablespoon of wheat bran to your hot cereal will give you even more fiber. If you add 1–2 teaspoons of ground flaxseed to your cereal, you will have a source of omega-3 fats.

This breakfast has only half a fruit serving because 2 teaspoons of brown sugar (or white sugar or honey) are added to the hot cereal.

If you don't add any sugar to your cereal, or if you use a low-calorie sweetener, you may have a whole fruit serving (as shown with most of the other breakfasts).

Packaged single servings of oatmeal are fast and easy, but most have a lot of sugar added. Look for the ones that say "plain" or "natural" and check that sugar is not listed in the ingredients.

You may want to mix half a package of instant unsweetened oatmeal with half a package of one of the flavored oatmeals. This way you'll get a lightly sweetened oatmeal and you can add a half fruit serving.

Studies show that people who eat breakfast are healthier. For more information about the importance of breakfast, go to "Newsletters" at **mealsforgoodhealth.com**.

Your Breakfast Menu	Large Meal (370 calories)	Small Meal (250 calories)
Hot cereal	1 1/2 cups cooked (6 tablespoons dry)	1 cup cooked (4 tablespoons dry)
Brown sugar	2 teaspoons	2 teaspoons
Raisins	1 1/2 tablespoons	1 tablespoon
Skim or 1 percent milk	3/4 cup	1/2 cup

BREAKFAST 6

French Toast

Two tablespoons of light syrup or 2 teaspoons of diet jam are the same as 1 tablespoon of regular syrup.

A pinch of nutmeg or cinnamon is a nice addition to the French toast dip.

French toast is quick and easy to make.

This breakfast is served with fruit and syrup. If you don't have fresh strawberries, any other kind of fruit, either fresh, frozen or canned, will do.

French Toast

Makes six pieces of toast.

2 large eggs

1/4 cup of skim milk

Pinch of salt, if desired

6 slices of bread

Each French Toast
Calories: 96
Carbohydrate: 14.5 g
Protein: 5.0 g
Fat: 2.4 g

1. In a medium bowl, beat the eggs with a fork. Add the milk and salt.
2. Dip the bread into the egg and milk.
3. On a hot non-stick pan, cook both sides until golden brown. See page 56 if you don't have a non-stick pan.

	Per Large Meal	Per Small Meal
Carbohydrates	63 g	42 g
Protein	15.5 g	10.5 g
Fat	7.5 g	5.0 g
Saturated Fat	2.0 g	1.3 g
Cholesterol	219 mg	146 mg
Fiber	6.8 g	4.7 g
Sodium	501 mg	335 mg
Vitamin A	103 µg	69 µg
Folic Acid	68 µg	47 µg
Vitamin C	43 mg	34 mg
Potassium	436 mg	307 mg
Calcium	141 mg	95 mg
Iron	3.6 mg	2.4 mg

Your Breakfast Menu	Large Meal (370 calories)	Small Meal (250 calories)
French toast	3 slices	2 slices
Jam	1 tablespoon, or 2 tablespoons diet jam	2 teaspoons, or 4 teaspoons diet jam
Strawberries	5 large	4 large

SMALL MEAL

BREADKFAST 7

Muffin & Yogurt

Go to **mealsforgoodhealth.com**
for other muffin recipes.

Bran Muffins

Makes twelve medium muffins.

1 cup flour

1 1/2 teaspoons baking powder

1/2 teaspoon baking soda

1/2 teaspoon salt

1/4 cup unsweetened applesauce

2 tablespoons margarine or vegetable oil

1/4 cup packed brown sugar

1/4 cup molasses (or honey)

1 egg

1 cup skim milk

1 1/2 cups wheat bran

1/2 cup raisins

Each Bran Muffin
Calories: 143
Carbohydrate: 29 g
Protein: 3.8 g
Fat: 2.8 g

Large bought muffins can have as much as five teaspoons of hidden fat. Try making these delicious, low-fat muffins. They only have 1/2 teaspoon of added fat in each muffin.

Instead of a muffin, you may have a low-fat granola bar.

Instead of yogurt, have a 1/2 cup of low-fat milk. For the small meal, you could have a slice of low-fat cheese instead of yogurt. See page 84, Lunch 7, to learn more about choosing yogurt.

	Per Large Meal	Per Small Meal
Carbohydrates	51 g	51 g
Protein	16.1 g	9.1 g
Fat	13.3 g	4.0 g
Saturated Fat	6.6 g	0.7 g
Cholesterol	49 mg	20 mg
Fiber	6.1 g	6.1 g
Sodium	444 mg	270 mg
Vitamin A	134 µg	55 µg
Folic Acid	61 µg	56 µg
Vitamin C	66 mg	66 mg
Potassium	776 mg	749 mg
Calcium	517 mg	315 mg
Iron	2.2 mg	2.0 mg

1. In a medium bowl, mix flour, baking powder, soda and salt together.
2. In a large bowl combine applesauce, margarine and brown sugar. Stir with a wooden spoon until well mixed.
3. Beat in the molasses and the egg. Add the milk, then add the wheat bran.
4. Add the flour mixture to the large bowl. Then add the raisins. The mixture will be wet.
5. Spoon into an ungreased, non-stick muffin tin. If you don't have a non-stick tin, use paper cups or lightly grease your muffin tin. Bake in a 400°F oven for 20 to 25 minutes. They are ready when a toothpick put into the center of a muffin comes out clean.

Your Breakfast Menu	Large Meal (370 calories)	Small Meal (250 calories)
Bran Muffin	1	1
Low-fat fruit yogurt with low-calorie sweetener	1/2 cup	1/2 cup
Orange	1 small (2 to 3 inches)	1 small (2 to 3 inches)
Piece of cheese	1 ounce	–

BREAKFAST 8

Raisin Toast & Cheese

Instead of two slices of raisin toast, you could have one raisin scone or one hot cross bun.

Instead of the cheese shown, you may choose a cup of milk.

Grapefruit treat:
A nice way to have grapefruit is to sprinkle it with a bit of cinnamon and low-calorie sweetener. Then, microwave it for thirty seconds or broil it until warm.

Raisin toast makes a nice change. You may want to have half your toast with the cheese broiled on top. The rest of the toast can be served with a thin spread of jam, which has fewer calories than margarine.

The large meal can include either 1 ounce of brick cheese or 1 1/2 slices of cheese. If you choose low-fat cheese, you will get less fat. Check the label:

- A low-fat block cheese or cheese slice has 20 percent or less milk fat (20% M.F.).
- Regular-fat cheese has about 35 percent milk fat.

Enjoy half a grapefruit or choose one serving of another type of fruit, such as:

- half a medium apple (or 1 small)
- a peach
- half a small banana
- an orange

When you eat breakfast, even a piece of fruit or a slice of toast, you have more energy. Your body will also "switch on" and start using up your fat. Please go back to pages 14-16 for more tips to help you lose weight and gain health.

	Per Large Meal	Per Small Meal
Carbohydrates	55 g	36 g
Protein	12.6 g	8.7 g
Fat	11.9 g	8.0 g
Saturated Fat	6.6 g	4.4 g
Cholesterol	31 mg	21 mg
Fiber	3.7 g	2.8 g
Sodium	721 mg	482 mg
Vitamin A	100 µg	73 µg
Folic Acid	42 µg	33 µg
Vitamin C	47 mg	47 mg
Potassium	392 mg	310 mg
Calcium	260 mg	178 mg
Iron	2.3 mg	1.5 mg

Your Breakfast Menu	**Large Meal** (370 calories)	**Small Meal** (250 calories)
Raisin toast	3 slices	2 slices
Jam or jelly	1 teaspoon, or	–
	2 teaspoons of diet jam	–
Cheese slice	1 1/2 slices (1 ounce)	1 slice
Grapefruit	1/2	1/2

BREAKFAST 9

Waffle & Hot Cocoa

Store-bought frozen waffles make an easy, quick breakfast. The plain waffles have fewer calories. For a treat, you may want to choose waffles that have blueberries or other fruits added.

Have your waffle with a small amount of jam, honey or syrup, as shown in the box below.

There is one fruit serving included with this breakfast.

Light hot cocoa mixes come in a variety of flavors. They are made with skim milk powder and are sweetened with a low-calorie sweetener. Choose a light hot cocoa mix that has fewer than fifty calories in a 3/4 cup serving. Check the label.

Choose one of these instead of 1 cup of light hot cocoa:
- *1/2 cup low-fat milk*
- *1/2 cup diet yogurt*
- *1 slice (1 ounce) low-fat cheese*

	Per Large Meal	Per Small Meal
Carbohydrates	68 g	52 g
Protein	9.3 g	6.6 g
Fat	9.0 g	3.0 g
Saturated Fat	2.2 g	0.9 g
Cholesterol	96 mg	49 mg
Fiber	1.6 g	1.1 g
Sodium	710 mg	417 mg
Vitamin A	272 µg	124 µg
Folic Acid	14 µg	9 µg
Vitamin C	3 mg	3 mg
Potassium	633 mg	571 mg
Calcium	194 mg	146 mg
Iron	3.3 mg	2.5 mg

Your Breakfast Menu	**Large Meal** (370 calories)	**Small Meal** (250 calories)
Waffle	2	1
Margarine or butter	1 teaspoon	–
Syrup (or, honey or jam)	1 tablespoon, or	1 tablespoon, or
	2 tablespoons light syrup	2 tablespoons light syrup
Grapes	3/4 cup	3/4 cup
Light hot cocoa	1 cup (14 g package)	1 cup (14 g package)

SMALL MEAL

Lunch Meals

- **each large lunch has 520 calories**
- **each small lunch has 400 calories**

LUNCH 1

Sandwich with Milk

Here's a quick recipe for tuna or salmon filling. It makes enough for at least four sandwiches.
Mix together:
- *184 g can water-packed tuna*
- *1 tablespoon light mayonnaise*
- *1–2 teaspoons relish*
- *1 stick of finely chopped celery*

Don't put margarine or mayonnaise on your bread when you use this filling.

	Per Large Meal	Per Small Meal
Carbohydrates	83 g	67 g
Protein	31.5 g	22.6 g
Fat	8.7 g	6.0 g
Saturated Fat	1.4 g	1.0 g
Cholesterol	27 mg	15 mg
Fiber	5.3 g	4.4 g
Sodium	1689 mg	1024 mg
Vitamin A	582 μg	581 μg
Folic Acid	117 μg	99 μg
Vitamin C	123 mg	123 mg
Potassium	1691 mg	1524 mg
Calcium	411 mg	386 mg
Iron	4.1 mg	2.8 mg

There are many nutritious fillings for sandwiches, for example, roast beef (as shown in the photograph), chicken or turkey breast, lean meat, cheese, egg or fish. Choose water-packed canned fish or leftover mashed fish for your sandwiches. Salmon and sardines are good choices because the fish bones give you calcium and the fish provides heart healthy omega-3 fats.

Each sandwich shown is made with 2 teaspoons of light mayonnaise. You may choose to use no fat at all, or use only 1 teaspoon of relish or mustard, or 1 tablespoon of salsa, which are all low in fat.

If you want a chopped filling, you can add celery, onion, green pepper or any other vegetable, with just a little light mayonnaise. Add your mayonnaise to the filling instead of on your bread.

Include some kind of vegetable on the side, such as three radishes, a stalk of celery, or a few slices of tomato or green pepper.

Cantaloupe or any other type of fruit serving is good with this meal.

You can have a cup of skim milk, 1 percent milk or butter-milk, or 3/4 cup of light yogurt. If you would like a slice of cheese as an extra in your sandwich, don't have the milk to drink.

Your Lunch Menu	Large Meal (520 calories)	Small Meal (400 calories)
Meat sandwich	1 1/2 sandwiches	1 sandwich
• bread, light rye	• 3 slices	• 2 slices
• roast beef	• 2 ounces	• 1 ounce
• light mayonnaise	• 1 tablespoon	• 2 teaspoons
• lettuce	• 2 large leaves	• 2 large leaves
Radishes	3	3
Cantaloupe	1/2 a small one	1/2 a small one
Skim or 1 percent milk	1 cup	1 cup

SMALL MEAL

LUNCH 2

Beans & Toast

For a change, choose canned spaghetti instead of beans.

Check the labels of light ice cream bars. Choose the ones that have fewer than 50 calories. One regular ice cream bar will have at least 150 calories.

Instead of a light ice cream bar or home-made Frozen Yogurt Bar, you could have a 1/2 cup of milk.

Open a can of brown beans, warm them up and serve a portion of them, as shown, with toast and fresh vegetables. Remove any chunks of pork fat from the baked beans, or buy beans canned only in tomato sauce.

For a change from toast, eat your beans with bannock (see page 115 for recipe) or another type of bread.

If you don't have any celery, choose a sliced tomato or 1/2 cup of tomato or vegetable juice.

Look for ice cream bars that are marked light or low-fat, and that are sweetened with a low-calorie sweetener. They taste good and have calcium. If you want to make your own low-fat and low-sugar frozen treats, try these Frozen Yogurt Bars.

Frozen Yogurt Bars

Makes eight bars.

2 cups plain skim milk yogurt

1/2 teaspoon diet (sugar-free) fruit flavored drink crystals

1. Mix the crystals with the yogurt.
2. Pour into containers and freeze.

Each Frozen Yogurt Bar
Calories: 33
Carbohydrate: 5 g
Protein: 3.1 g
Fat: 0.1 g

	Per Large Meal	Per Small Meal
Carbohydrates	102 g	76 g
Protein	24.4 g	18.3 g
Fat	6.9 g	6.4 g
Saturated Fat	1.4 g	1.2 g
Cholesterol	2 mg	2 mg
Fiber	31.7 g	21.8 g
Sodium	1766 mg	1258 mg
Vitamin A	84 µg	73 µg
Folic Acid	141 µg	111 µg
Vitamin C	19 mg	15 mg
Potassium	1580 mg	1201 mg
Calcium	359 mg	295 mg
Iron	3.2 mg	2.8 mg

Your Lunch Menu	Large Meal (520 calories)	Small Meal (400 calories)
Canned baked beans	1 1/4 cups	3/4 cup
Toast	2 slices	2 slices
Margarine	1 teaspoon	1 teaspoon
Celery sticks	2 stalks	2 stalks
Frozen Yogurt Bar	1	1

SMALL MEAL

Chicken Soup & Bagel

Grandmother was right. Chicken soup is good medicine when you are feeling ill; and when you are feeling well.

Instead of both salmon and cream cheese, a bagel could be served with any of these:

- *1 ounce or one thin slice of cheese or meat such as ham or turkey. Limit high-fat meats like bologna and salami.*
- *1/4 cup canned fish*
- *2 teaspoons peanut butter*

	Per Large Meal	Per Small Meal
Carbohydrates	94 g	69 g
Protein	19.4 g	15.1 g
Fat	9.1 g	8.3 g
Saturated Fat	2.8 g	2.7 g
Cholesterol	38 mg	27 mg
Fiber	5.2 g	5.1 g
Sodium	2062 mg	1707 mg
Vitamin A	489 µg	488 µg
Folic Acid	116 µg	92 µg
Vitamin C	86 mg	86 mg
Potassium	781 mg	732 mg
Calcium	193 mg	176 mg
Iron	4.3 mg	3.0 mg

Canned soup or packaged soups are quick and easy. Add a handful of frozen vegetables for added nutrition. Cream soups have extra fat, so choose them less often. Try this recipe.

Chicken Rice Soup

Makes 7 1/2 cups.

Each 1-1/2 cup Chicken Rice Soup
Calories: 99
Carbohydrate: 18 g
Protein: 3.7 g
Fat: 1.2 g

2 medium carrots, chopped

1 medium onion, chopped

2 stalks of celery, chopped

1/4 cup rice (uncooked)

1 package (60 g) of dried chicken noodle soup mix

1 teaspoon (or half cube) chicken bouillon mix

1/4 teaspoon of dried dill

6 cups of water

1. Chop carrots, onion and celery.
2. Put all ingredients in a medium pot.
3. Cover and gently boil for about 20 minutes, until the carrots are cooked. Stir occasionally.

The bagel shown here is served with light cream cheese, and salmon, tomato and onion. For a change try smoked salmon (lox).

Your Lunch Menu	Large Meal (520 calories)	Small Meal (400 calories)
Chicken Rice Soup	1 1/2 cups	1 1/2 cups
Soda crackers	2	2
Bagel	1 (or 3 slices bread)	1/2 (or 1-1/2 slices bread)
Light cream cheese (20% fat)	1 tablespoon	1 tablespoon
Canned pink salmon	2 tablespoons	2 tablespoons
Tomato	1/2 a medium	1/2 a medium
Sliced onion	3 slices	3 slices
Orange	1 small (2 to 3 inches)	1 small (2 to 3 inches)

LUNCH 4

Macaroni & Cheese

If you would like a slice of bread thinly spread with butter with this lunch, cut the macaroni and cheese by 1/4 cup.

If you don't have any green or yellow beans, choose raw vegetables such as:
- *up to three celery stalks*
- *one medium carrot*
- *one large tomato*
- *half a medium cucumber*

Boxed macaroni and cheese is an easy choice for lunch. After cooking the macaroni, just add milk and the powdered cheese. You don't need to add any butter or margarine.

For extra calcium, you can mix in 2 tablespoons of skim milk powder with the macaroni and cheese.

If you would prefer a home-made macaroni and cheese, there is a recipe with Dinner 18.

Green or yellow beans can be fresh, frozen or canned. Steam or microwave vegetables, or very lightly boil them. Overcooked vegetables lose important vitamins and minerals as well as good flavor.

	Per Large Meal	Per Small Meal
Carbohydrates	**91 g**	**76 g**
Protein	**17.7 g**	**13.7 g**
Fat	**10.1 g**	**6.9 g**
Saturated Fat	5.3 g	3.9 g
Cholesterol	8 mg	6 mg
Fiber	7.6 g	6.8 g
Sodium	1243 mg	788 mg
Vitamin A	70 µg	50 µg
Folic Acid	15 µg	15 µg
Vitamin C	19 mg	19 mg
Potassium	692 mg	591 mg
Calcium	234 mg	189 mg
Iron	4.9 mg	3.9 mg

Your Lunch Menu	**Large Meal** (520 calories)	**Small Meal** (400 calories)
Macaroni & Cheese (no added fat)	1 cup	3/4 cup
Green beans	1 cup	1 cup
Green olives	3	1
Apple	1 (3-inch)	1 (3-inch)

SMALL MEAL

LUNCH 5

Toasted Cheese & Tomato Sandwich

Coleslaw from a restaurant or store-bought has a lot of fat in the dressing. Try this low-fat recipe.

Mayonnaise has about the same calories as margarine or butter. Light mayonnaise or calorie-reduced margarine has one-third the calories, or less. These light brands have fewer than 45 calories in 1 tablespoon.

	Per Large Meal	Per Small Meal
Carbohydrates	76 g	59 g
Protein	22 g	16.6 g
Fat	17.7 g	13.6 g
Saturated Fat	7.3 g	5.1 g
Cholesterol	34 mg	24 mg
Fiber	9.4 g	7.0 g
Sodium	1089 mg	789 mg
Vitamin A	579 µg	532 µg
Folic Acid	115 µg	90 µg
Vitamin C	56 mg	44 mg
Potassium	1258 mg	1034 mg
Calcium	461 mg	371 mg
Iron	4.2 mg	3.1 mg

Coleslaw

Makes 6 1/2 cups.

4 cups shredded cabbage

4 medium carrots, grated

4 stalks of celery, finely chopped

1 small onion

1 tablespoon sugar

3 tablespoons low-fat (light) mayonnaise

1/4 cup vinegar

1/4 teaspoon garlic powder

Salt and pepper, to taste

Each 1/2 cup Coleslaw
Calories: 36
Carbohydrate: 6 g
Protein: 0.7 g
Fat: 1.2 g

1. Chop the cabbage in fine strips, grate the carrots, and finely chop the celery and onion. Mix these together in a large bowl.
2. In a small bowl, mix the mayonnaise, sugar, vinegar, garlic powder, salt and pepper. Add to the cabbage. Mix well.
3. Cover and put in the fridge. This will keep well for one week.

Your Lunch Menu	Large Meal (520 calories)	Small Meal (400 calories)
Toasted cheese & tomato sandwich	1 1/2 sandwiches	1 sandwich
• bread	• 3 slices	• 2 slices
• cheese	• 1 1/2 slices	• 1 slice
• tomato	• 1 large	• 1 medium
• lettuce	• 1–2 leaves	• 1–2 leaves
• mayonnaise	• 2 teaspoons	• 2 teaspoons
Coleslaw (or raw veggies)	1/2 cup	1/2 cup
Cherries	1/2 cup	1/2 cup
Skim or 1 percent milk	1/2 cup	1/2 cup

SMALL MEAL

LUNCH 6

Cold Plate with Soup

Shop for low-fat cheese:
- *1% cottage cheese*
- *block cheese that is 20% M.F. (milk fat) or less*

The vegetable soup may be dried or canned. Dried soups usually have fewer calories than canned.

Soda crackers are very low in fat. They have little fat compared with snack crackers. Choose the unsalted soda crackers.

Instead of the small bun shown, you could have a slice of bread, half an English muffin, one small bran muffin, four melba toast or six soda crackers (plus the two with your soup).

If you don't usually eat cottage cheese, have a slice of hard cheese instead.

You may choose 14 hot pepper rings (pickled) instead of a dill pickle. Or, for a less salty choice, choose sliced cucumber in vinegar.

Have a fruit serving with your cold plate, either fresh, frozen or canned (in water or juice).

	Per Large Meal	Per Small Meal
Carbohydrates	76 g	65 g
Protein	40.6 g	25.1 g
Fat	9.1 g	6.2 g
Saturated Fat	3.4 g	2.2 g
Cholesterol	10 mg	5 mg
Fiber	7.3 g	6.9 g
Sodium	2834 mg	2294 mg
Vitamin A	120 µg	107 µg
Folic Acid	134 µg	116 µg
Vitamin C	45 mg	45 mg
Potassium	1051 mg	937 mg
Calcium	242 mg	169 mg
Iron	4.6 mg	4.0 mg

Your Lunch Menu	Large Meal (520 calories)	Small Meal (400 calories)
Vegetable soup (packaged)	1 cup	1 cup
Soda crackers	3	–
Cold plate		
• 1 percent cottage cheese	1 cup	1/2 cup
• peaches	2 halves	2 halves
• dill pickle	1 medium	1 medium
• lettuce	5 large leaves	5 large leaves
• tomato	1 medium	1 medium
• green onions	4	4
• whole wheat bun (small)	1	1
• Arrowroot biscuits	2	2

LUNCH 7

Peanut Butter & Banana Sandwich

Yogurt ideas:

- *Mix one container of plain skim milk yogurt with one container of regular fruit yogurt. It will then have 1 1/2 teaspoons of sugar in 1/2 cup.*
- *Make up your own fruit yogurt simply by adding fruit to a low-fat yogurt. Add a low-calorie sweetener if you like.*

	Per Large Meal	Per Small Meal
Carbohydrates	**79 g**	**63 g**
Protein	**19.6 g**	**15.2 g**
Fat	**16.4 g**	**11.5 g**
Saturated Fat	3.3 g	2.4 g
Cholesterol	5 mg	4 mg
Fiber	6.2 g	5.2 g
Sodium	1085 mg	904 mg
Vitamin A	883 µg	883 µg
Folic Acid	103 µg	87 µg
Vitamin C	22 mg	22 mg
Potassium	1213 mg	1131 mg
Calcium	296 mg	273 mg
Iron	3.8 mg	2.9 mg

I never seem to get tired of peanut butter and banana sandwiches.

Make each sandwich without margarine or butter, and with 1 tablespoon of peanut butter and half a banana.

Peanut butter also goes well with jam or honey. Limit the jam or honey to 1 teaspoon, or 2 teaspoons of diet jam. Still have half a banana or any other fruit choice on the side.

My dad's favorite Sunday lunch is a peanut butter and onion sandwich. If you like onions, use as many as you like on your peanut butter sandwich. Have a fruit on the side.

Choose vegetable juice and carrot sticks as shown, or other fresh vegetables.

Regular fruit-flavored yogurt has 3 teaspoons of sugar added in 1/2 a cup. Using a yogurt made with a low-calorie sweetener will cut out this extra sugar.

You may have either 1/2 cup of light yogurt or 1/2 cup of low-fat milk.

Your Lunch Menu	Large Meal (520 calories)	Small Meal (400 calories)
Peanut butter & banana sandwich	1 1/2 sandwiches	1 sandwich
• white bread	• 3 slices	• 2 slices
• peanut butter	• 1 1/2 tablespoons	• 1 tablespoon
• small banana	• 1/2	• 1/2
Carrot sticks	1 medium carrot	1 medium carrot
Tomato or vegetable juice	1/2 cup	1/2 cup
Low-fat yogurt (sweetened with low-calorie sweetener)	1/2 cup	1/2 cup

SMALL MEAL

LUNCH **8**

Pita Sandwich

Fill your pita with lots of vegetables and a little protein.

Try these vegetables in your pita:
- lettuce and tomatoes
- bean sprouts and alfalfa sprouts
- grated carrots
- chopped green pepper

Try one of these in your pita instead of the cheese and ham
(portions are for the large meal):
- 1/2 cup water-packed tuna or salmon
- 3/4 cup 1 percent cottage cheese
- 1/3 cup chopped firm tofu
- 1/2 cup hummus
- 1 1/2 tablespoons sesame tahini spread
- 1 1/2 tablespoons peanut butter

Hummus can be made by blending canned chick peas.
Add lemon, garlic and spices, such as cumin, for best flavor.
You can also buy hummus as a dry mix; you need only to add
water to the dry mix.

Include milk or some other milk food, such as yogurt or a diet
ice cream bar.

	Per Large Meal	Per Small Meal
Carbohydrates	82 g	60 g
Protein	24.8 g	21.6 g
Fat	12.9 g	8.9 g
Saturated Fat	6.0 g	4.0 g
Cholesterol	44 mg	32 mg
Fiber	5.1 g	3.8 g
Sodium	863 mg	733 mg
Vitamin A	474 µg	439 µg
Folic Acid	107 µg	103 µg
Vitamin C	58 mg	51 mg
Potassium	1041 mg	836 mg
Calcium	392 mg	327 mg
Iron	3.9 mg	3.3 mg

Your Lunch Menu	**Large Meal** (520 calories)	**Small Meal** (400 calories)
Pita	1 (6-inch)	1 (6-inch)
• lettuce	1/4 cup chopped	1/4 cup chopped
• tomato	1/2 a medium	1/2 a medium
• bean sprouts	1/4 cup	1/4 cup
• carrots	1/2 a small	1/2 a small
• green pepper	2 tablespoons chopped	2 tablespoons chopped
• ham, lean	1 ounce	1 ounce
• cheddar cheese, shredded	3 tablespoons	2 tablespoons
Plums	2 medium	1 medium
Skim or 1 percent milk	1/2 cup	1/2 cup
Gingersnap cookies	2	–

SMALL MEAL

LUNCH 9

Chef's Salad, Bun & Soup

Whether you're at home or in a restaurant, you may want to have a salad with a bun and soup for your lunch.

A chef's salad, Caesar salad or Greek salad is easy to make. A chef's salad recipe follows, and there is a recipe for Greek salad on page 207. Or try the Avocado Salad found in the "Newsletter" section at **mealsforgoodhealth.com**. You can toss these salads with low-fat croutons and a store-bought "oil-free", "fat-free" or "calorie-reduced" dressing. Low-fat salad dressings should have fewer than 10 calories per tablespoon. Regular salad dressings often have more than 100 calories per tablespoon.

When you order a salad in a restaurant, ask for low-fat salad dressing on the side. If you don't, your salad will come soaked in fat and will be just as greasy as your neighbor's order of fries.

In restaurants, salads often are served with greasy garlic toast. Ask for a plain bun or dried bread sticks instead.

	Per Large Meal	Per Small Meal
Carbohydrates	70 g	56 g
Protein	24.5 g	22.1 g
Fat	18.8 g	12.1 g
Saturated Fat	4.8 g	3.2 g
Cholesterol	267 mg	252 mg
Fiber	7.8 g	6.8 g
Sodium	1470 mg	485 mg
Vitamin A	769 µg	745 µg
Folic Acid	122 µg	119 µg
Vitamin C	92 mg	92 mg
Potassium	1106 mg	970 mg
Calcium	141 mg	102 mg
Iron	4.2 mg	3.5 mg

Chef's Salad

Makes two servings.

2 cups chopped lettuce

2 medium tomatoes, sliced

Other vegetables, such as onions, green peppers, celery, radishes or carrots

1 apple, sliced

2 slices of cheese or meat

2 eggs, hard boiled and sliced

2 tablespoons croutons

1. Toss vegetables and apple. Place the meat or cheese and egg on top.
2. Add an oil-free salad dressing and croutons.

Each serving Chef's Salad
Calories: 256
Carbohydrate: 31 g
Protein: 19.1 g
Fat: 7.6 g

Your Lunch Menu	Large Meal (520 calories)	Small Meal (400 calories)
Cream of celery or tomato soup (made with water)	1 cup	clear broth (optional)
Wheat crackers	2 halves	–
Chef's Salad	1 serving (half of recipe)	1 serving (half of recipe)
Oil-free salad dressing	1 tablespoon	1 tablespoon
Bun, white	1 small	1 small
Margarine	1/2 teaspoon	1/2 teaspoon

LUNCH 10

French Onion Soup

*For other soup recipes see: Recipes and Newsletters at **mealsforgoodhealth.com***

Another way to make this soup is to use one package of dried onion soup mix (the kind with dried flakes of onion). This package of soup would replace the bouillon and the onions.

There is a lot of salt in soup mix and bouillon. Look for low-salt varieties.

Regular-fat cheese is used in this recipe—as low-fat cheese does not broil as nicely.

French onion soup is a meal all on its own. It's easy to make at home with this recipe.

Other hearty soups are canned split pea or bean soup, or home-made hamburger soup (see recipe on page 114). Or you could have a bowl of cream soup made with milk and toss in some vegetables.

French Onion Soup

Makes four servings.

4 cups water

2 medium onions, thinly sliced

4 packets (or 4 cubes) beef bouillon mix

4 slices white bread, toasted

4 ounces of Swiss or mozzarella cheese (this is equal to four slices of cheese, each 4-inch square and 1/8-inch thick)

Each serving French Soup
Calories: 228
Carbohydrate: 23 g
Protein: 12.8 g
Fat: 9.2 g

1. Add the bouillon mix, water and sliced onions to a pot. Bring to a boil. Turn down heat and simmer for 15 minutes until onions are soft.
2. Pour soup into four oven-proof bowls.
3. Cut dry toast into cubes. Put one full slice of cubed toast onto each bowl of soup. Place a slice of Swiss cheese on top of the bread.
4. Broil in the oven until the cheese bubbles.

	Per Large Meal	Per Small Meal
Carbohydrates	76 g	59 g
Protein	18.9 g	16.0 g
Fat	18.8 g	14.7 g
Saturated Fat	6.7 g	5.9 g
Cholesterol	28 mg	28 mg
Fiber	9.7 g	8.0 g
Sodium	1273 mg	1042 mg
Vitamin A	202 µg	154 µg
Folic Acid	158 µg	151 µg
Vitamin C	23 mg	23 mg
Potassium	941 mg	794 mg
Calcium	409 mg	380 mg
Iron	2.7 mg	1.9 mg

Your Lunch Menu	Large Meal (520 calories)	Small Meal (400 calories)
French Onion Soup	1 serving	1 serving
Tossed salad	large	large
Oil-free salad dressing	1 tablespoon	1 tablespoon
Rye bread	1 slice	–
Margarine	1 teaspoon	–
Pear	1	1

Dinner Meals

- **each large dinner has 730 calories**
- **each small dinner has 550 calories**

DINNER 1

Baked Chicken & Potato

*The following recipe for **Chicken Spice Mix** makes enough for many meals. Put two teaspoons oregano and one teaspoon of thyme, paprika, pepper and chili powder in a jar with a tight lid. Mix well. Sprinkle the mixture on the skinless chicken.*

It is important to remove the fatty chicken skin. Sprinkle on this salt-free and sugar-free Chicken Spice Mix – see sidebar. Or, roll the chicken in a store-bought shake-and-bake coating, or baste lightly with your favorite barbecue sauce.

Bake the chicken pieces on a rack so the extra fat drip offs. Bake in a 350°F oven for about an hour. Or grill on the barbecue. Or cook in a stick-free pan with a small amount of water and barbecue sauce. Chicken is cooked when the meat moves easily when pierced with a fork, and the juices have no trace of pink. Or cook to 170°F measured with an instant read thermometer.

Compare the fat and sugar content of fast-food chicken with this home-baked chicken, which has the skin and fat removed.

The breast of baked chicken shown in the **small** meal photograph has:

- 1 teaspoon of fat
- no sugar

The same piece of chicken, if battered and deep-fried at a fast-food restaurant, would have:

- 4 teaspoons of fat
- 3 teaspoons of sugar or starch

Have your potato plain, with 1 teaspoon of butter or margarine, or with 1 tablespoon of light or fat-free sour cream.

The vegetables that go with this meal are celery, radishes and frozen mixed vegetables.

Easy-to-make pudding from a box:
Light puddings sweetened with a low-calorie sweetener are a good source of calcium and have fewer calories than regular puddings. Make your puddings with skim milk. Butterscotch pudding has been chosen for this meal, but you can choose your own favorite flavor.

Instead of frozen mixed vegetables, you could choose one of these sweet vegetables:
- *peas*
- *carrots*
- *parsnips*
- *beets*
- *turnips*
- *squash (orange)*

Store-bought light puddings or light mousses should have fewer than 75 calories in a 1/2 cup serving.

Instead of pudding, you could choose 1 cup low-fat milk.

	Per Large Meal	Per Small Meal
Carbohydrates	108 g	82 g
Protein	59.5 g	44.0 g
Fat	7.7 g	5.6 g
Saturated Fat	2.6 g	1.9 g
Cholesterol	127 mg	88 mg
Fiber	13.1 g	10.8 g
Sodium	605 mg	563 mg
Vitamin A	279 µg	275 µg
Folic Acid	96 µg	82 µg
Vitamin C	55 mg	42 mg
Potassium	2358 mg	1825 mg
Calcium	270 mg	247 mg
Iron	7.0 mg	5.2 mg

Your Dinner Menu	Large Meal (730 calories)	Small Meal (550 calories)
Baked chicken	1 1/2 breasts (5 ounces, cooked)	1 breast (3 1/2 ounces, cooked)
Baked potato, with skin	1 large	1 medium
Light sour cream	1 1/2 tablespoons	1 tablespoon
Mixed vegetables	3/4 cup	3/4 cup
Radishes	3	3
Celery	1 stalk	1 stalk
Light butterscotch pudding	1/2 cup	1/2 cup

SMALL MEAL

DINNER 2

Spaghetti & Meat Sauce

Spaghetti and meat sauce is an easy-to-make favorite. I often double this recipe and freeze the extra. When you have no dinner planned, it's great to have a container of spaghetti sauce in the freezer.

Whether you use regular or lean ground beef, it is important to brown it first and drain off as much fat as you can.

You can remove extra fat by adding hot water to the browned meat, then draining it off.

*For a meatless spaghetti sauce, make this recipe but do not add the meat or the tomato paste. For protein for the large meal, sprinkle 5 tablespoons of shredded cheese or 3 tablespoons of sunflower seeds on top of your spaghetti and sauce. Use a little less for the small meal. Or try Karen's Vegetarian Spaghetti Sauce found at **mealsforgoodhealth.com***

Store-bought spaghetti sauces (in jars or cans) can have a lot of added fat, sugar or starch. For example, one cup of some meatless spaghetti sauces have 2 teaspoons of added fat and 4 teaspoons of added sugar or starch. If you do buy spaghetti sauce, look for one labeled as light.

Spaghetti Meat Sauce

Makes 6 cups of sauce.

Each 1 cup Meat Sauce
Calories: 183
Carbohydrate: 15 g
Protein: 16.4 g
Fat: 7.3 g

1 pound lean ground beef

1 medium onion, chopped

28 ounce (796 ml) can of tomatoes

1 cup water

1 small tin (156 ml) tomato paste

1/2 teaspoon garlic powder

2 bay leaves (remove before serving)

1/2 teaspoon chili powder

1 teaspoon oregano

1 teaspoon basil

1/4 teaspoon paprika

1/8 teaspoon ground cinnamon

1/8 teaspoon ground cloves

1 cup chopped vegetables, such as green pepper, celery or mushrooms

1. Brown the ground beef. Drain off as much fat as you can.
2. Add the rest of the ingredients.
3. Bring to a boil, then turn down heat. Cover and simmer for 2 hours. Stir every now and then so the sauce doesn't stick. Add extra water if it gets too thick.
4. Serve over hot spaghetti, with Parmesan cheese if you like.

Use regular or whole wheat spaghetti.
Add dry spaghetti to a pot of boiling water, stir and cook for about 10 minutes. Drain off water.

Carrots are served with this meal.

Use an oil-free salad dressing. See Lunch 9, page 88, for more about low-fat salad dressings.

Light gelatin has few calories and is a good dessert choice after a big meal. It takes only a few minutes to make, but must be left in the fridge for about two hours to set. If you find the boxed diet gelatins are costly, try this easy-to-make recipe.

Light Gelatin

Makes 2 cups.

1 envelope unflavored gelatin

1/2 package regular Kool-Aid or Freshie

1 cup cold water

1 cup boiling water

Low-calorie sweetener equal to 1/4 cup of sugar (use a bit less or more, to suit your taste)

Each 1/2 cup Light Gelatin
Calories: 14
Carbohydrate: 2 g
Protein: 1.5 g
Fat: 0 g

Whipped Gelatin is a variation you may want to try (see Dinner 10, page 131). When you whip the gelatin, you will get 4 cups instead of 2.

Another low-calorie dessert is store-bought "No sugar added" popsicles.

1. Soften the unflavored gelatin in 1/2 cup cold water.
2. Add the Kool-Aid or Freshie and 1 cup boiling water. Stir until gelatin is all mixed in.
3. Add 1/2 cup cold water and low-calorie sweetener.
4. Chill until firm (about 2 hours).

	Per Large Meal	Per Small Meal
Carbohydrates	113 g	91 g
Protein	42.5 g	30.0 g
Fat	14.1 g	9.6 g
Saturated Fat	4.2 g	2.6 g
Cholesterol	51 mg	30 mg
Fiber	11.3 g	8.9 g
Sodium	972 mg	545 mg
Vitamin A	1213 µg	1074 µg
Folic Acid	128 µg	110 µg
Vitamin C	44 mg	30 mg
Potassium	1735 mg	1237 mg
Calcium	386 mg	271 mg
Iron	9.6 mg	7.0 mg

Your Dinner Menu	Large Meal (730 calories)	Small Meal (550 calories)
Spaghetti	1 3/4 cups	1 1/2 cups
Meat sauce	1 1/4 cups	3/4 cup
Cooked carrots	1/2 cup	1/2 cup
Salad	medium	medium
Oil-free salad dressing	1 tablespoon	1 tablespoon
Skim or 1 percent milk	3/4 cup	1/2 cup
Light gelatin	1/2 cup	1/2 cup

SMALL MEAL

DINNER 3

Fish with Rice

Low-fat fishes include sole, pickerel, red snapper and haddock. Blue fish is a medium-fat fish. The high-fat fishes include trout and red (sockeye) salmon. Eat a bit less of the high-fat fishes.

These spices go well with fish:
- *allspice*
- *basil*
- *cajun spice*
- *curry*
- *dill*
- *mustard*
- *oregano*
- *parsley*
- *thyme*

One cup of cooked brown rice has 50 fewer calories than one cup of cooked white rice and adds more fiber.

Light soy sauce is a good low-fat topping for rice instead of butter or margarine.

The fish may be broiled or baked in an oven at 350°F. The fish shown in the photograph is red snapper, and it was baked and lightly brushed with margarine. Fish can also be microwaved, steamed, grilled on the barbecue, or fried in a non-stick pan (with just a little fat). If you are cooking fish in your oven or on your barbecue, you can wrap it in tin foil. Fish is good with spices, onions and vegetables wrapped up in the foil too.

Before cooking fish:
Poke it with a fork and pour 2 tablespoons of lemon juice or a 1/4 cup of dry wine over it. Sprinkle it with your favorite spices. You may also want to roll the fish in bread crumbs or flour.

The secret to great tasting fish is to not overcook it. Fish is cooked when it flakes easily.

Cooking rice:
Cook rice according to directions on the package.

When you are in a hurry, you can use instant rice. It cooks in just 5 minutes.

Vegetables:
This meal is served with peas, a sweet vegetable, and with yellow or green beans, which are less-sweet. For extra flavor without many calories, mix a small can of mushrooms in with the peas.

Other less-sweet vegetables are:
- summer squash or spaghetti squash
- broccoli
- cauliflower
- spinach

See page 131 for a list of low-calorie vegetables.

Fruit Milkshake

Makes 2 cups.

1 cup skim milk

1/2 cup frozen or fresh fruit of your choice

1 tablespoon sugar or equal amount of low-calorie sweetener

Each cup of Fruit Milkshake
Calories: 81
Carbohydrate: 16 g
Protein: 4.4 g
Fat: 0.3 g

This milkshake is easy to make. It is so thick and good, you won't believe it's made with skim milk and not with ice cream.

Turn to page 38 to learn how much low-calorie sweetener to use instead of sugar.

1. Pour the milk in a mixing bowl or a blender. Place your mixing bowl or blender in your freezer for half an hour.
2. Take your bowl or blender out of the freezer. Add the fruit and sugar (or low-calorie sweetener) to the milk. Mix in the blender for about thirty seconds. If you don't have a blender, mix in your bowl with beaters until thick and frothy. Serve right away.

	Per Large Meal	Per Small Meal
Carbohydrates	**100 g**	**78 g**
Protein	**61.1 g**	**43.9 g**
Fat	**9.9 g**	**8.0 g**
Saturated Fat	1.9 g	1.6 g
Cholesterol	81 mg	55 mg
Fiber	13.9 g	12.3 g
Sodium	299 mg	262 mg
Vitamin A	187 µg	167 µg
Folic Acid	79 µg	72 µg
Vitamin C	93 mg	92 mg
Potassium	1775 mg	1440 mg
Calcium	318 mg	285 mg
Iron	4.1 mg	3.5 mg

Your Dinner Menu	Large Meal (730 calories)	Small Meal (550 calories)
Fish with lemon slice	6 ounces, cooked	4 ounces, cooked
Margarine (to cook fish)	1 teaspoon	1 teaspoon
Brown rice	1 1/4 cups	3/4 cup
Green peas	1/2 cup	1/2 cup
Yellow beans	1 cup	1 cup
Fruit Milkshake	1 cup	1 cup
Kiwi	1 medium (3-inch)	1 medium (3-inch)

SMALL MEAL

DINNER 4

Roast Beef

Here's a great way to cook your roast:
- Place your roast on a rack in a roasting pan, with no lid. Add 1 cup of water to the pan. Sprinkle with pepper but not salt (salt tends to dry out the roast). Bake in a hot 500°F oven for 30 minutes.
- Reduce the oven heat to 275°F. Leave roast uncovered and cook for another 1 1/2 hours for a 5-pound (2.4 kg) roast.

Once the roast beef has been removed from the pan, skim the fat from the meat juice with a spoon. Or, put some ice cubes into the meat juice, and the fat will stick to the ice cubes. With a spoon, take out the ice cubes. If you have time, you can let the juice cool and the fat in the juice will harden and can then easily be removed. You can serve the meat juice as it is, or thicken it into a gravy as below.

The lower cost, medium-tender, low-fat cuts of roast beef are:
- *"round" cuts, such as inside round and outside round*
- *"loin" cuts, such as sirloin or sirloin tip.*

Roast beef can also be cooked in a table-top "slow-cooker" pot.

You can also buy low-fat gravy mix packages, to which you add only water. These should have fewer than 10 calories in a serving. Look for one that says it is low in calories; it may be called "au jus" (with juice).

Choose light bouillon cubes to reduce salt.

Do not use plain water for the 2 cups of liquid, or your gravy will taste plain.

Gravy Flavorings:
- *canned mushrooms*
- *hot sauce*
- *pepper*
- *Worcestershire sauce*
- *garlic*
- *light soy sauce*

Low-Fat Gravy

Makes 2 1/3 cups.

Each 1/4 cup Low-Fat Gravy
Calories: 19
Carbohydrate: 6 g
Protein: 0.8 g
Fat: 0.1 g

2 packets (or 2 cubes) beef bouillon mix (use chicken bouillon if making gravy for poultry)

1 teaspoon onion soup mix (or 1 tablespoon finely chopped onion)

2 cups liquid made from either fat-free meat juice, potato water or other vegetable water

1/4 cup flour, cornstarch or instant blending flour

1/2 cup cold water

1. Add the beef bouillon and onion soup mix to your 2 cups of hot liquid.
2. In a jar, mix the flour or cornstarch with the cold water. Tighten the lid and shake well. Add this mixture slowly to the hot juice and cook at medium heat. Stir it often with a whisk until thick and smooth, about five minutes.

The oven-roasted potatoes are peeled and cooked for an hour on a non-stick or greased rack or pan. Coat your potatoes with an oil-free Italian dressing or sprinkle with spices.

Have beets as shown, or carrots, turnips, corn, peas, or any other vegetable.

For dessert have the rhubarb with either a lower-fat ice cream (made with 10 percent B.F., or butter fat), sherbet, frozen yogurt or ice milk. If you don't want dessert, drink a cup of milk with your meal.

Enjoy horseradish with your roast beef; it is a low-fat relish.

Vegetables such as carrots are also good baked on a rack in the oven.

This rhubarb is nice as a dessert or as a snack served warm on a piece of toast.

The low-calorie sweetener in the drink mix adds enough sweetness.

Stewed Rhubarb

Makes 1 3/4 cups.

2 tablespoons water

4 cups rhubarb (fresh or frozen)
  1-inch pieces

1/2 teaspoon sugar-free drink mix
  (either strawberry or raspberry)

Dash of cinnamon

Each cup of Stewed Rhubarb
Calories: 66
Carbohydrate: 13 g
Protein: 2.6 g
Fat: 0.6 g

1. Put the rhubarb and water in a heavy pot and cook at low temperature on the stove. Add water as needed. Cook for about 15 minutes, or until soft.
2. Take off the stove and, while still warm, add sugar-free drink mix and cinnamon.
3. Have it warm or cool. Keep in the fridge.

	Per Large Meal	Per Small Meal
Carbohydrates	**92 g**	**73 g**
Protein	**53.8 g**	**35.5 g**
Fat	**19.0 g**	**14.6 g**
Saturated Fat	7.1 g	5.6 g
Cholesterol	124 mg	83 mg
Fiber	13.6 g	12.1 g
Sodium	392 mg	268 mg
Vitamin A	86 µg	86 µg
Folic Acid	164 µg	149 µg
Vitamin C	57 mg	48 mg
Potassium	2828 mg	2306 mg
Calcium	361 mg	353 mg
Iron	6.0 mg	4.3 mg

Your Dinner Menu	Large Meal (730 calories)	Small Meal (550 calories)
Roast beef	5 ounces, cooked	3 ounces, cooked
Horseradish	1 tablespoon	1 tablespoon
Baked (or pickled) onions	3 small or 1 medium	3 small or 1 medium
Roasted potatoes	1 large	1 medium
Low-Fat Gravy	1/4 cup	2 tablespoons
Beets	1/2 cup	1/2 cup
Salad	small	small
Oil-free Italian salad dressing	1 tablespoon	1 tablespoon
Stewed Rhubarb	1 cup	1 cup
Ice Cream	1/3 cup	1/3 cup

SMALL MEAL

DINNER 5

Dinner Cold Plate

*T*wo ounces of regular fat cheese (32 percent fat) is about equal in calories to:
- *3 ounces of low-fat (17 percent fat) cheese*
- *1 1/4 cups of 1 percent cottage cheese*

This is one of my mom's favorite light and easy meals. She buys a bag of pre-washed spinach and mixes it all in the bag. The ***Meals for Good Health*** **CD/DVD** (see order information on page 2) includes a demonstration by myself and my son making a dinner spinach salad that includes heart healthy fats.

You may wish to replace the cheese shown in the photograph with low-fat cheese (see side bar).

Fish choices include salmon, tuna, sardines, shrimp, crab or lobster, all canned in water. Red (sockeye) salmon is included with this meal. You may want to choose pink salmon, which is a bit lower in fat than red. You may have one slice of cold meat instead of fish.

Your starch may be a bun, two slices of bread, or eight melba toast. Add any number and variety of fresh vegetables.

For dessert have this rice pudding. The pudding is not too creamy but has a nice cinnamon flavor and is the right sweetness. It is good warm or cold.

Rice Pudding

Makes four 1-cup servings.

Each cup Rice Pudding
Calories: 212
Carbohydrate: 41 g
Protein: 7.6 g
Fat: 2.4 g

1 egg

1 1/2 cups skim milk

2 tablespoons sugar (or low-calorie sweetener, if desired)

1/2 teaspoon ground cinnamon

1/2 teaspoon vanilla

2 cups cooked rice (brown or white)

1/4 cup raisins

1. In a large bowl, beat the egg, milk, sugar or sweetener, cinnamon and vanilla. Use a spoon or whisk.
2. Stir in rice and raisins.
3. Pour into lightly greased baking dish.
4. Bake at 350°F for forty-five minutes or until the center is set.

*Instead of the rice pudding you could have a light pudding, a small dish of sherbet or frozen yogurt, or a serving of fresh fruit or Banana Bread (visit **mealsforgoodhealth.com** for recipe).*

	Per Large Meal	Per Small Meal
Carbohydrates	**75 g**	**64 g**
Protein	**40.2 g**	**31.4 g**
Fat	**32.1 g**	**20.4 g**
Saturated Fat	14.9 g	8.4 g
Cholesterol	134 mg	90 mg
Fiber	7.1 g	6.6 g
Sodium	1042 mg	829 mg
Vitamin A	346 µg	228 µg
Folic Acid	91 µg	83 µg
Vitamin C	65 mg	65 mg
Potassium	1024 mg	930 mg
Calcium	774 mg	540 mg
Iron	3.7 mg	3.3 mg

Your Dinner Menu	Large Meal (730 calories)	Small Meal (550 calories)
Dinner Cold Plate		
• lettuce or spinach	a plateful	a plateful
• tomato	1/2 medium	1/2 medium
• green & red pepper	5 rings	5 rings
• cucumber	4 thick slices	4 thick slices
• radishes	2 large	2 large
• red salmon, water-packed	1/2 cup	1/2 cup
• cheddar cheese	2 ounces	1 ounce
• bun, whole wheat	1	1
• margarine	1/2 teaspoon	–
Rice Pudding	1 cup	3/4 cup

SMALL MEAL

Hamburger Soup & Bannock

The great thing about this soup is that it is a meal all in one. Freeze any leftovers.

Hamburger Soup

Makes 10 cups.

1 pound hamburger (or 1 pound chopped or ground wild meat)	**Each 1-1/2 cups Hamburger Soup** Calories: 226 Carbohydrate: 26 g Protein: 16.1 g Fat: 7.4 g

1 medium onion, chopped

1 clove garlic or 1/4 teaspoon garlic powder

19 ounce (540 ml) can tomatoes

10 ounce (284 ml) can tomato soup

1 teaspoon Worcestershire sauce

1/8 teaspoon pepper

4 cups water

4 packets (or 4 cubes) beef bouillon mix

3 medium carrots, peeled and sliced

1 cup chopped cabbage

12 ounce (341 ml) can kernel corn

1/4 cup dry macaroni

1. Brown the hamburger meat. Drain off as much fat as you can.
2. Add the onions and garlic, and cook at low heat until onions are soft.
3. Add the tomatoes, tomato soup, Worcestershire sauce, pepper, water and bouillon mix.
4. Bring to a boil, cover and simmer for half an hour.
5. Add the vegetables and macaroni. Cover and simmer for another half an hour.

If you've never had bannock—try it. This bread is made without yeast and is easy to make. It is cooked in the oven or in a cast-iron frying pan. Instead of the piece of bannock shown here, you may choose two slices of bread or one bun.

Bannock

Makes one 9-inch bannock (or ten pieces).

3 cups flour

1 tablespoon baking powder

1 teaspoon salt

1 tablespoon sugar

1/4 cup margarine or other fat, melted, or vegetable oil

1 cup skim milk

Each piece of Bannock
Calories: 190
Carbohydrate: 31.5 g
Protein: 4.8 g
Fat: 4.8 g

You can use any type of fat when you make bannock. I prefer to use margarine because it gives the bannock a nice golden color.

I use milk instead of water in the bannock because the milk helps in the rising, adding flavor and good nutrition, too.

Bannock is nice when 1/4 cup of raisins or blueberries are added to the batter.

1. In a large bowl, mix together the flour, baking powder, salt and sugar.
2. Mix the melted margarine with the milk. Add this mixture to the flour. Mix with a spoon to make a soft dough.
3. Put this on a floured board or table. With your hands, flatten and shape it until it is one 9-inch piece.
4. Put on a non-stick or lightly greased cookie sheet. Bake in the oven at 375°F for twenty minutes, until lightly browned.
5. Cut into ten pieces.

Here's how you can cook bannock on your stove or campfire. Make the bannock batter with only 2 tablespoons of margarine or other fat. Add an extra tablespoon of milk to keep the batter soft. Into the cast-iron pan, add 2 tablespoons fat and fry the bannock for ten minutes on each side at low heat. This fried bannock has the same amount of fat as it does when baked.

	Per Large Meal	Per Small Meal
Carbohydrates	111 g	80 g
Protein	27.4 g	22.7 g
Fat	20.9 g	16.1 g
Saturated Fat	5.2 g	4.2 g
Cholesterol	35 mg	34 mg
Fiber	8.9 g	7.8 g
Sodium	2187 mg	1823 mg
Vitamin A	757 µg	692 µg
Folic Acid	111 µg	103 µg
Vitamin C	116 mg	116 mg
Potassium	1125 mg	1048 mg
Calcium	269 mg	198 mg
Iron	6.1 mg	4.6 mg

Your Dinner Menu	Large Meal (730 calories)	Small Meal (550 calories)
Hamburger Soup	1 1/2 cups	1 1/2 cups
Bannock	2 pieces	1 piece
Margarine	1 teaspoon	1 teaspoon
Orange	1 large	1 large

115

SMALL MEAL

DINNER 7

Beans & Wieners

For extra flavor, try adding one of these to your beans and wieners:

- *1 tablespoon salsa sauce*
- *1 teaspoon Worcestershire sauce*
- *1/4 teaspoon hot sauce*

Beef or pork wieners are high in fat and salt. This meal makes a few wieners go a long way. The beans are low-fat and give you protein and fiber.

Try a lower fat wiener such as a turkey wiener. A tofu wiener is a vegetarian choice and is even lower in fat. Tofu is made from soy beans, which are low in fat and high in protein. You will usually find tofu and tofu wieners in the vegetables section of your grocery store.

Beans and Wieners

Makes 2 1/4 cups.

	Each 1 cup of Beans and Wieners
14 ounce (398 ml) can brown beans (in tomato sauce)	Calories: 333 Carbohydrate: 40 g Protein: 15.1 g Fat: 15.1 g
3 regular wieners	

1. Place the beans in a pot or cooking dish.
2. Cut the wieners in slices and add to the beans.
3. Heat on the stove or in a microwave oven.

Serve Beans and Wieners with toast and a tossed salad, with chocolate mousse for dessert.

This dessert recipe is easy to make, and it is thick and delicious.

Chocolate Mousse

Makes six 1/2-cup servings.

1 package (4 servings) of light chocolate instant pudding mix

1 1/2 cups skim milk

1 cup frozen whipped topping, thawed until soft

Each 1/2 cup Chocolate Mousse
Calories: 82
Carbohydrate: 11 g
Protein: 2.7 g
Fat: 3.1 g

You may want to make this chocolate mousse with regular pudding instead of light. By doing so, you will add an extra 2 1/2 teaspoons of sugar to each serving.

1. Pour the 1 1/2 cups skim milk into a medium bowl and add the pudding mix. Beat with a whisk or an electric mixer until thickened (about two minutes).
2. Fold in the thawed whipped topping until well blended (or if you want a marbled look, fold in the topping gently and don't fully mix).
3. Pour into six dessert dishes, and serve.

	Per Large Meal	Per Small Meal
Carbohydrates	**94 g**	**75 g**
Protein	**30.0 g**	**22.4 g**
Fat	**31.8 g**	**22.8 g**
Saturated Fat	10.9 g	7.5 g
Cholesterol	47 mg	32 mg
Fiber	26.0 g	18.7 g
Sodium	2554 mg	1900 mg
Vitamin A	147 µg	120 µg
Folic Acid	187 µg	163 µg
Vitamin C	20 mg	17 mg
Potassium	1497 mg	1175 mg
Calcium	304 mg	252 mg
Iron	3.3 mg	2.7 mg

Your Dinner Menu	Large Meal (730 calories)	Small Meal (550 calories)
Beans & Wieners	1 1/2 cups	1 cup
Toast	2 small or 1 regular slice	2 small or 1 regular slice
Margarine	1/2 teaspoon	–
Tossed salad	large	large
Oil-free salad dressing	1 tablespoon	1 tablespoon
Chocolate Mousse	1/2 cup	1/2 cup

SMALL MEAL

DINNER 8

Steak & Potato

Look for "round" or "loin" cuts of beef. These are lowest in fat and are less costly.

Trim off all the fat.

On the barbecue, try not to let your meat burn. You can stop this by lightly spraying the coals with water to keep the flames down.

The simplest way to cook a steak is to barbecue or broil it, or fry it in a very hot, heavy frying pan with a bit of water. If frying in a pan, cover with a lid to reduce fat spraying out. Cook for only about four minutes on each side.

Tips to make your steak more tasty and tender:
- Marinade your meat for a few hours in Shish Kebob Marinade (see page 206)—then barbecue or broil it.
- Soak it for a few hours in canned tomatoes, wine, wine vinegar, beer or plain yogurt. Then fry the steak in a bit of broth or water, or barbecue or broil it.
- Brown the steak on the stove in a bit of beef broth or water. Add one can of tomatoes or 1 cup of salsa. Cover the pan and simmer for an hour.

Fresh mushrooms can be barbecued or broiled. Canned or fresh mushrooms can be cooked in a separate pan or added to the pan with the steak.

Serve the steak with Low-Fat Mashed Potatoes or with a boiled or baked potato.

Low-Fat Mashed Potatoes

Make low-fat mashed potatoes by mashing the potatoes and adding only milk, no butter or margarine. Add enough milk to make the potatoes creamy and smooth.

Spice Mix

Here is a spice mix you can make. Shake some on your meat, your potato or rice, and your vegetable.

2 teaspoons garlic powder
2 teaspoons dried lemon powder
1 teaspoon basil
1 teaspoon oregano
1 teaspoon ground pepper
1 teaspoon chili powder

Does your food taste bland without the extra shake of salt? If so, try some of these on your meat, potato or vegetables:
- *pepper*
- *parsley, lemon or lime (fresh or dried)*
- *onion powder*
- *garlic powder*
- *spices or herbs*
- *store-bought spice mixes*

Choose an oil-free or fat-free salad dressing for your salad.

Brussels sprouts are healthy mini-cabbages. If you don't have any, choose one of your own favorite vegetables.

Sherbet, frozen yogurt, ice milk and 10% B.F. ice cream have less fat than regular ice cream.

	Per Large Meal	Per Small Meal
Carbohydrates	**83 g**	**73 g**
Protein	**56.3 g**	**37.0 g**
Fat	**21.1 g**	**15.0 g**
Saturated Fat	8.0 g	5.4 g
Cholesterol	84 mg	53.4 mg
Fiber	8.1 g	7.3 g
Sodium	420 mg	378 mg
Vitamin A	132 µg	128 µg
Folic Acid	254 µg	246 µg
Vitamin C	82 mg	77 mg
Potassium	2147 mg	1729 mg
Calcium	172 mg	157 mg
Iron	5.3 mg	3.8 mg

Your Dinner Menu	Large Meal (730 calories)	Small Meal (550 calories)
Steak	5 ounces, cooked	3 ounces, cooked
Low-Fat Mashed Potatoes	1 cup	2/3 cup
Mushrooms	1/2 cup	1/2 cup
Brussels sprouts	3/4 cup	3/4 cup
Salad	large	large
Oil-free salad dressing	1 tablespoon	1 tablespoon
Sherbet	1/2 cup	1/2 cup

SMALL MEAL

DINNER *9*

Cheese Omelet

An omelet makes a great dinner. I cook a cheese omelet about once a week because it is easy and fast. It is okay to have eggs for a main meal once a week, as long as the eggs are eaten in place of meat.

Cheese Omelet

This is the recipe for the large meal. The small meal serving is the same, but it is made with just one egg.

2 eggs

1 ounce (or 1 slice) of cheese, cut into pieces

1. In a small bowl, beat the eggs. Pour into a non-stick pan.
2. Place the cheese on top.
3. Put a lid on and cook at low heat, for about 5 minutes.

To your broccoli, you may add 1 tablespoon of light cheese spread. This has the same calories as 1 teaspoon of butter or margarine.

For dessert, enjoy 1 or 2 oatmeal cookies. Or in place of an oatmeal cookie, you could have a plain cookie such as a digestive or ginger snap.

You can add an extra egg white to your omelet. An egg white has no cholesterol and only 20 calories. An egg yolk has 60 calories.

Try this in your omelet:
- *a sprinkle of dried or fresh dill or parsley*
- *1 tablespoon of finely chopped onion, green onion or chives.*

Oatmeal Cookies

Makes 36 cookies.

Each Oatmeal Cookie
Calories: 75
Carbohydrate: 13 g
Protein: 1.4 g
Fat: 2.0 g

1/3 cup margarine

3/4 cup packed brown sugar

1 egg

1/2 cup skim milk

1 teaspoon vanilla

1 cup flour

1 teaspoon baking powder

1 teaspoon baking soda

1 teaspoon ground cinnamon

1 1/2 cups rolled oats

1 cup raisins

1. In a large mixing bowl, mix together the margarine, brown sugar and egg. Beat with a wooden spoon until smooth. Beat in the milk and vanilla.
2. In a medium bowl, mix together the flour, baking powder, baking soda, cinnamon, and rolled oats.
3. Add the flour and oats to the large bowl. Stir well. Add the raisins and stir again.
4. Drop small spoonfuls of batter onto a non-stick baking sheet. Batter will be sticky. Bake in a 375°F oven for about ten minutes or until golden.

*T*o keep your non-stick pans and non-stick cookie sheets in good shape, use a plastic spatula or plastic spoon rather than a metal one. Store your non-stick pans so that other pots aren't scratching them. I wrap mine in tea towels.

	Per Large Meal	Per Small Meal
Carbohydrates	73 g	58 g
Protein	36.5 g	28.7 g
Fat	36.3 g	25.7 g
Saturated Fat	13.7 g	11.1 g
Cholesterol	483 mg	262 mg
Fiber	11.9 g	11.3 g
Sodium	1176 mg	1001 mg
Vitamin A	560 µg	403 µg
Folic Acid	207 µg	187 µg
Vitamin C	173 mg	173 mg
Potassium	1081 mg	958 mg
Calcium	510 mg	468 mg
Iron	6.2 mg	5.1 mg

Your Dinner Menu	Large Meal (730 calories)	Small Meal (550 calories)
Cheese Omelet	1 large	1 small
Toast	2 slices	2 slices
Margarine	2 teaspoons	1 teaspoon
Broccoli	2 cups of pieces	2 cups of pieces
Light cheese spread	1 tablespoon	1 tablespoon
Oatmeal cookies	2	1

SMALL MEAL

DINNER 10

Ham & Sweet Potato

For this meal, buy a cooking ham. Look for one that has the least amount of fat. Put the ham on a rack in a roasting pan. Bake your ham for about twenty-five minutes per pound (1 1/2 hours per kg) at 325°F. If you are using a thermometer, cook to 160°F.

You can flavor and decorate the top of your ham by pushing about one dozen whole cloves into the outside of the ham. I usually put slices of pineapple on top of the ham for the last half-hour of the cooking.

Mustard can be enjoyed with your ham.

A sweet potato (or yam) has different vitamins and minerals than a regular potato, and it's nice for a change. Like orange squash and carrots, sweet potato is rich in vitamin A— important for healthy eyes. Since your oven is on, cook it like a regular baked potato. Poke it with a fork and cook until tender. Bake it for an hour.

Try these Seasoned Bread Crumbs sprinkled on your cauliflower.

Hams have a small amount of either sugar or honey added. "Honey" ham does not have more sugar than regular ham.

Sweet potato can also be cooked by:
- *microwaving it at high for ten minutes*
- *boiling it with the skin on (take off the skin, once it is cooked).*

You can also sprinkle the Seasoned Bread Crumbs on other vegetables and on baked dishes.

Seasoned Bread Crumbs

Makes just over 1 cup.

You can buy bread crumbs, or make your own by crushing dry bread and adding spices.

	Each teaspoon
1 cup bread crumbs	Calories: 9
2 tablespoons Parmesan cheese	Carbohydrate: 2 g
1 tablespoon dried parsley	Protein: 0.4 g
1 teaspoon oregano	Fat: 0.2 g
1/2 teaspoon garlic powder	
1/8 teaspoon pepper	

Mix ingredients together. Store Seasoned Bread Crumbs in the fridge.

All vegetables are good choices but some, such as cauliflower, broccoli and yellow beans, have a higher amount of fiber and water. This makes them low in calories.

Low-calorie vegetables:

- asparagus
- green or yellow beans
- bean sprouts
- broccoli
- Brussels sprouts
- cabbage
- cauliflower
- celery
- cucumber
- eggplant
- fiddle heads
- leafy greens, such as lettuce and spinach
- marrow
- mushrooms
- okra
- onions
- green or red peppers
- radishes
- summer and spaghetti squash
- tomato
- zucchini

Whipped Gelatin

Makes 4 cups.

14 calories per cup
Carbohydrate: 2 g
Protein: 1.5 g
Fat: 0 g

1 package light gelatin of your favorite flavor

1. Make the gelatin according to the directions on the box (or use the recipe on page 99).
2. Remove the gelatin from the fridge after about forty-five minutes. It should be as thick as an unbeaten egg white. Beat the gelatin with a beater until it is foamy and has doubled in size.
3. Put it back in the fridge until firm.

	Per Large Meal	Per Small Meal
Carbohydrates	**90 g**	**77 g**
Protein	**49.0 g**	**35.3 g**
Fat	**21.2 g**	**12.6 g**
Saturated Fat	6.3 g	3.8 g
Cholesterol	87 mg	54 mg
Fiber	10.3 g	8.8 g
Sodium	2399 mg	1506 mg
Vitamin A	2433 µg	1839 µg
Folic Acid	143 µg	130 µg
Vitamin C	119 mg	107 mg
Potassium	2077 mg	1673 mg
Calcium	425 mg	406 mg
Iron	4.1 mg	3.1 mg

Your Dinner Menu	Large Meal (730 calories)	Small Meal (550 calories)
Baked ham	1 thick slice (5 ounces, cooked)	1 thin slice (3 ounces, cooked)
Pineapple, packed in juice	3 rings, no juice	3 rings, no juice
Sweet potato	1 large	1 medium
Margarine	2 teaspoons	1 teaspoon
Cauliflower	2 cups	2 cups
Seasoned Bread Crumbs	1 teaspoon	1 teaspoon
Skim milk or 1 percent milk	1 cup	1 cup
Whipped Gelatin	1 cup	1 cup

SMALL MEAL

DINNER 11

Beef Stew

Beef stew served with potatoes and bread is an old favorite. This recipe is lower in fat, as it uses lean meat and only a small amount of added fat.

Vegetables that go well in a stew include turnips, yellow and green beans, carrots and peas. If you are in a rush, you can use frozen mixed vegetables in this recipe in place of the fresh vegetables.

Double the recipe if you want to make more to freeze for another day.

For dessert have a fruit serving.

If you are in a hurry, try this:
Open a can of beef stew, put it in a pot and add some frozen or cooked vegetables. Cook until heated.

Beef Stew

Recipe makes 7 cups.

1 tablespoon margarine or oil
2 medium onions, chopped
2 cloves garlic, chopped (or 1/2 teaspoon garlic powder)
1 pound stewing beef, remove any fat and chop (cut in the size of a "dice")
2 tablespoons flour
2 packets (or 2 cubes) beef bouillon mixed in 2 cups hot water
1 bay leaf (remove before serving)
2 large stalks of celery, sliced
3 medium carrots, sliced
2 cups other fresh vegetables (or frozen mixed vegetables)
1/8 teaspoon pepper
1/4 cup dry wine (or wine vinegar)

Each cup of Beef Stew
Calories: 165
Carbohydrate: 16 g
Protein: 13.2 g
Fat: 5.3 g

1. Place the margarine, onions and garlic in a heavy pot. Cook and stir on medium heat until the onions become clear. Stir often so they do not burn.
2. Add the meat and stir it until it is cooked on the outside (about five minutes). Sprinkle the flour over the onion and meat mixture, and stir until the flour disappears.
3. Take the pot off the heat while you add the rest of the ingredients. Stir. Return to heat. Bring to a boil and then turn the heat down to low. Cover and simmer for about an hour. Stir occasionally.
4. If you are using frozen mixed vegetables instead of fresh vegetables, add them just at the end and simmer for ten minutes.

North African Stew and Couscous

For a change, you may want a spicier stew. Try a North African beef stew. This stew would commonly be made with onions, carrots, turnips, tomatoes, zucchini, pumpkin and squash. When you cook the meat, add 1 teaspoon of each of the following: turmeric, cinnamon and cumin (or try 1 tablespoon of curry powder, instead), and 1 teaspoon of chili powder. Make this stew a day ahead so that the spice taste is best.

Instead of having this stew with bread and potatoes, you can serve it with couscous. Serve 1 1/4 cups couscous for the large meal and 1 cup for the small meal. Couscous is made from wheat and can be bought in all major food stores. It looks like rice and tastes like noodles. It is easy and quick to make because you just boil it in water. Serve the stew and couscous with mint tea.

	Per Large Meal	Per Small Meal
Carbohydrates	**115 g**	**93 g**
Protein	**35.6 g**	**27.8 g**
Fat	**16.9 g**	**11.0 g**
Saturated Fat	4.0 g	2.8 g
Cholesterol	45 mg	34 mg
Fiber	13.4 g	11.2 g
Sodium	1208 mg	931 mg
Vitamin A	1104 µg	1421 µg
Folic Acid	163 µg	144 µg
Vitamin C	127 mg	117 mg
Potassium	2695 mg	2215 mg
Calcium	160 mg	133 mg
Iron	5.8 mg	4.7 mg

Your Dinner Menu	**Large Meal** (730 calories)	**Small Meal** (550 calories)
Beef Stew	2 cups	1 1/2 cups
Boiled potatoes	1 large	1 medium
Bread	1 slice	1 slice
Margarine	1 teaspoon	1/2 teaspoon
Sliced cucumbers	1/2 medium cucumber	1/2 medium cucumber
Cantaloupe or melon	2 slices	2 slices

SMALL MEAL

DINNER 12

Fish & Chips

You could have store-bought chicken nuggets with your fries and vegetables instead of fish sticks.

- *for the large meal you could have 7 chicken nuggets (140 grams)*
- *for the small meal you could have 5 chicken nuggets (95 grams).*

Compare the calories of 10 french fries:
- *fried in oil from a restaurant – 160 calories.*
- *frozen fries baked in the oven – 90 calories.*
- *Baked Low-fat Fries – 60 calories.*

Bought packages of potato seasonings have sugar and salt. If you want to use these, use less than a tablespoon for this whole recipe.

Squash:
The orange squash shown in the photograph is an acorn squash. There are many kinds of squash. For example you may want to try spaghetti squash, one of the less sweet squashes.

This is an easy meal prepared with ready-made frozen fish sticks and frozen french fries. Bake them in the oven on a cookie sheet. The portions of fish sticks and the frozen french fries are kept small because of the fat in them. This meal has a lot less fat than battered fish and french fries that are deep-fried in oil.

Look for brands of fish sticks that are labeled low in fat. These are often made with less oil or a lighter batter.

You can also make Baked Low-Fat Fries at home using the recipe below. The photograph shows the store-bought frozen french fries, not these home-made ones.

Baked Low-Fat Fries

Makes 45 fries (15 fries for each potato).

For 12 Fries
Calories: 77
Carbohydrate: 16 g
Protein: 2.9 g
Fat: 0.2 g

3 small potatoes

1 egg white

1 teaspoon spices (choose from the spices listed on page 102 such as curry, dill or cajun spice)

1. Wash and peel the potatoes.
2. Cut into fry-size pieces or chunks.
3. In a small bowl, mix the egg white and spices with a fork.
4. Dip the potato pieces into the mixture.
5. Bake the potato pieces on a greased non-stick cookie sheet at 400°F. Cook for about thirty minutes, turning them every ten minutes.

With this meal, have one vegetable serving of squash, peas, carrots, corn, turnips or parsnips.

Here is how I cooked the squash shown in the photograph: cut a squash in half and place the cut side down on a cookie sheet. Bake in the oven with the fish and fries. Bake for half an hour, or until tender.

Try this light Jellied Vegetable Salad. It is colorful and tasty and low in calories. The lime gelatin gives it a nice green colour.

Jellied Vegetable Salad

Makes 2 1/2 cups (five servings).

1 package light lime gelatin

1 1/2 cups boiling water

2 tablespoons lemon or lime juice

1/2 cup finely chopped radish

1/2 cup finely chopped celery

1/2 cup finely chopped cabbage

1 tablespoon chopped fresh or dried parsley

Each 1/2 cup Jellied Vegetable Salad
Calories: 15
Carbohydrate: 2 g
Protein: 1.4 g
Fat: 0.2 g

Jellied Vegetable Salad can be a low-calorie vegetable choice with any lunch or dinner meal. A half cup has only 20 calories.

For a lightly salted and less sweet flavor in the Jellied Vegetable Salad, try this:
- *add one packet of light chicken bouillon mix, or one bouillon cube, to the boiling water.*

1. In a medium bowl, place the gelatin powder. Add the boiling water and stir until the gelatin is mixed in. Add the lemon juice. Put this mixture in the fridge.
2. Chop all the vegetables. Once the mixture in the fridge is slightly thickened (about forty-five minutes), stir in all the vegetables.
3. Chill until set (about another hour).

	Per Large Meal	Per Small Meal
Carbohydrates	**100 g**	**79 g**
Protein	**26.8 g**	**19.3 g**
Fat	**27.1 g**	**19.2 g**
Saturated Fat	9.1 g	6.4 g
Cholesterol	152 mg	101 mg
Fiber	7.8 g	86.8 g
Sodium	1195 mg	904 mg
Vitamin A	428 µg	412 µg
Folic Acid	86 µg	72 µg
Vitamin C	48 mg	45 mg
Potassium	1570 mg	1296 mg
Calcium	104 mg	91 mg
Iron	3.9 mg	3.1 mg

Your Dinner Menu	Large Meal (730 calories)	Small Meal (550 calories)
Fish sticks	6 sticks or 3 wedges	4 sticks or 2 wedges
Oven-baked frozen french fries	20	14
Ketchup	1 tablespoon	1 tablespoon
Squash	1/2 cup	1/2 cup
Jellied Vegetable Salad	1/2 cup	1/2 cup
Plum	1 medium	1 medium

SMALL MEAL

DINNER 13

Sausages & Corn Bread

Zucchini is also nice cooked in a pan with a teaspoon of margarine or oil and chopped onion and garlic. To this you can add one or two other vegetables, such as:
- *canned or fresh chopped tomatoes*
- *green pepper*
- *eggplant*

Add water to the pan, if needed. Sprinkle parmesean cheese on top.

Sausages are high in fat. Here are the best ways to cook them to remove some of the fat. First poke them several times so the fat can drain out.
- broil on a rack, or barbecue
- boil for 10 minutes, then bake in the oven until brown
- microwave sausages on a rack

Fill up on vegetables. Zucchini is a low-calorie vegetable that is easy to prepare by slicing and steaming. If you boil zucchini, it will get soggy. Sprinkle it with Seasoned Bread Crumbs (see recipe on page 130).

Use the coleslaw recipe in Lunch 5 on page 80. A 1/2 cup skim milk could replace the light ice cream bar.

Corn Bread or Corn Muffins

**Makes an 8-inch square pan
(12 pieces) or 12 muffins.**

3/4 cup cornmeal

1 1/4 cups skim milk

1 cup flour

1 tablespoon baking powder

1/2 teaspoon salt

1/4 cup sugar

1 egg, slightly beaten

**3 level tablespoons shortening, butter or margarine,
melted**

Each piece of Corn Bread
Calories: 126
Carbohydrate: 20 g
Protein: 3.2 g
Fat: 3.5 g

For a change, here are some starches that could take the place of two pieces of corn bread:
- *2 cups canned kernel corn or 2 small cobs of corn*
- *1 1/4 cup rice*

1. In a medium bowl, mix together the cornmeal and milk. Set aside for five minutes.
2. In a large bowl, mix together the flour, baking powder, salt and sugar.
3. In a small bowl, mix the slightly beaten egg and the melted fat. Add this to the cornmeal mixture.
4. Add the liquid mixture to the flour mixture. Stir until combined. Pour into an 8-inch square pan or muffin tin. Use a non-stick pan, or grease your pan lightly.
5. Bake in a 400°F oven for about twenty minutes (15 minutes for muffins), or until lightly browned.
6. Cut into twelve pieces (about 3-inches by 2-inches).

	Per Large Meal	Per Small Meal
Carbohydrates	**84 g**	**74 g**
Protein	**21.0 g**	**17.5 g**
Fat	**36.2 g**	**22.8 g**
Saturated Fat	9.9 g	6.6 g
Cholesterol	85 mg	67 mg
Fiber	7.0 g	6.6 g
Sodium	1144 mg	851 mg
Vitamin A	617 µg	492 µg
Folic Acid	86 µg	82 µg
Vitamin C	26 mg	26 mg
Potassium	1084 mg	1024 mg
Calcium	279 mg	245 mg
Iron	3.5 mg	3.1 mg

Your Dinner Menu	Large Meal (730 calories)	Small Meal (550 calories)
Sausages	4 small links	3 small links
Corn Bread	2 1/2 pieces	2 pieces
Margarine	2 teaspoons	–
Steamed zucchini	2 cups	2 cups
Seasoned Bread Crumbs	1 tablespoon	1 tablespoon
Coleslaw	1/2 cup	1/2 cup
Light fudge ice cream bar	1 bar	1 bar

SMALL MEAL

DINNER 14

Chili Con Carne

Chili freezes well. You can easily double the recipe for freezing.

Chili Con Carne

Makes 6 1/4 cups.

Each 1 cup Chili Con Carne	

Each 1 cup Chili Con Carne
Calories: 285
Carbohydrate: 33 g
Protein: 22.4 g
Fat: 7.6 g

1 pound lean ground beef

2 medium onions, chopped

28 ounce (796 ml) can kidney beans

10 ounce (284 ml) can tomato soup

1/8 teaspoon pepper

1/2 teaspoon chili powder

1 tablespoon vinegar

1/2 teaspoon Worcestershire sauce

1 cup chopped vegetables, such as celery or green pepper

1. In a large, heavy pot, brown the ground beef. Drain off as much fat as you can.
2. Add all the other ingredients to the pot.
3. Cover with a lid and cook for two to three hours on low heat. Stir every now and then so the chili doesn't stick. Add extra water if it gets too thick.

Serve the meal with brown or white rice.

Add a low-calorie vegetable such as yellow beans or green beans. Carrot sticks are served on the side.

Instead of 1/2 cup of rice:
- *1 1/2 slices of bread*
- *half a piece of bannock*
- *1 small potato*

For a dessert treat, try this tasty Baked Apple or have a serving of any other kind of fruit.

These baked apples have a lovely glaze because of the combination of brown sugar and butter. Margarine can be used instead, but butter makes the syrup thicker.

This recipe has less fat and sugar than a traditional baked apple. Regular sugar is used because low-calorie sweeteners tend to make the syrup in the apple too thin.

Baked Apple

Makes two baked apples.

2 medium apples

1 teaspoon butter or margarine

1 tablespoon brown sugar

1/4 teaspoon ground cinnamon

1/4 teaspoon lemon juice

Dash of nutmeg (if desired)

1 tablespoon raisins

Each Baked Apple
Calories: 142
Carbohydrate: 32 g
Protein: 0.5 g
Fat: 2.5 g

A baked apple helps satisfy a sweet tooth, and has less fat and sugar than a piece of apple pie.
- *A 3 1/2-inch piece of apple pie usually has about 7 teaspoons of added sugar and starch and 3 teaspoons of added fat.*
- *One of these Baked Apples has 1 1/2 teaspoons of added sugar and 1/2 teaspoon of added fat.*

*Visit **mealsforgoodhealth.com** for Peach Cobler, an alternative recipe to Baked Apple.*

1. Remove apple core, cutting from the top of the apple. Don't cut right through to the bottom. Prick apples with a fork.
2. In a small bowl, mix together the other ingredients and spoon into the apples.
3. Place apples on a dish and microwave them on high for one minute and twenty seconds, or until the apples are tender. Or place the apples in a pan with 2 tablespoons of water and bake in a 350°F oven for thirty minutes.

	Per Large Meal	Per Small Meal
Carbohydrates	117 g	93 g
Protein	38.5 g	26.6 g
Fat	14.3 g	10.6 g
Saturated Fat	5.4 g	4.0 g
Cholesterol	59 mg	41 mg
Fiber	20.4 g	16.3 g
Sodium	941 mg	648 mg
Vitamin A	940 µg	927 µg
Folic Acid	191 µg	135 µg
Vitamin C	45 mg	37 mg
Potassium	1617 mg	1261 mg
Calcium	184 mg	156 mg
Iron	9.3 mg	6.9 mg

Your Dinner Menu	**Large Meal** (730 calories)	**Small Meal** (550 calories)
Chili Con Carne	1 1/2 cups	1 cup
Rice	1/2 cup	1/3 cup
Green beans	1 cup	1 cup
Carrot sticks	1 medium carrot	1 medium carrot
Baked Apple	1	1

147

SMALL MEAL

DINNER 15

Perogies

Perogies and sour cream go together like hugs and kisses; but go for a light hug. Enjoy 1 tablespoon of light sour cream, or 2 tablespoons of fat-free sour cream with your perogies.
- *Fat-free sour cream has only 9 calories in a tablespoon.*
- *Light sour cream (7% fat) has 16 calories in 1 tablespoon.*
- *Regular sour cream (14% fat) has 32 calories in 1 tablespoon.*

Buy frozen perogies and enjoy a fast-food meal, at home. Perogies come with many fillings, such as cheese, potato, cottage cheese and even pizza.

First, fry onions at low heat in 1 teaspoon of fat. Then take the onions out of the pan so they don't get overcooked. Fry the perogies in the same pan until lightly browned. Another way to cook them is to boil them for ten minutes.

Instead of having a 2-ounce piece of garlic sausage (kolbasa) with the large meal, you could have:
- 1 cup of 1 percent cottage cheese
- 2 slices bologna, broiled or fried, without added fat

Instead of the beet soup, you may want to have 1 cup of cooked beets. Pickled beets have added sugar, so 1/2 cup of these would equal 1 cup of beet soup.

Easy Beet Soup

Makes 3 1/2 cups.

10 ounce (398 ml) can diced beets (unsweetened)

1 1/2 cups vegetable juice (such as V-8 juice)

2 cups chopped cabbage

1/4 teaspoon dried dill weed

Each 1 cup Easy Beet Soup
Calories: 64
Carbohydrate: 15 g
Protein: 2.1 g
Fat: 0.3 g

1. Place all ingredients in a pot.
2. Cover and simmer. Stir as it is cooking. It will take about fifteen minutes to cook.

Serve with a dab of low-fat sour cream and green onion tops.

For a low-calorie vegetable, have sauerkraut or a dill pickle. A low-salt alternative to sauerkraut or a pickle would be a small salad.

For dessert have one fresh peach. If you want canned peaches, have two halves with 2 tablespoons of juice. Choose fruit canned in water or juice. Have one plain cookie with your fruit. Plain bought cookies include arrowroot biscuits, digestives, raisin cookies (as shown in the photograph), ginger snaps, oatmeal cookies and Graham wafers.

	Per Large Meal	Per Small Meal
Carbohydrates	106 g	86 g
Protein	23.1 g	16.2 g
Fat	27.1 g	17.9 g
Saturated Fat	9.3 g	5.9 g
Cholesterol	49 mg	28 mg
Fiber	11.4 g	10.6 g
Sodium	2701 mg	2211 mg
Vitamin A	154 µg	154 µg
Folic Acid	108 µg	106 µg
Vitamin C	73 mg	71 mg
Potassium	1165 mg	1089 mg
Calcium	135 mg	123 mg
Iron	4.6 mg	4.2 mg

Your Dinner Menu	Large Meal (730 calories)	Small Meal (550 calories)
Perogies	6	4
Low-fat or fat-free sour cream	1 tablespoon	1 tablespoon
Cooked sliced onion in margarine	1/2 small onion 1 teaspoon	1/2 small onion 1 teaspoon
Garlic sausage	2 ounces	1 ounce
Easy Beet Soup	1 cup	1 cup
Cherry tomatoes	2, or 2 slices of tomato	2, or 2 slices of tomato
Sauerkraut	1/2 cup	1/2 cup
Peach	1	1
Plain cookie	1	1

151

SMALL MEAL

DINNER 16

Hamburger with Potato Salad

If you add 1/2 cup of fresh chopped mushrooms into your raw ground meat, this will keep your hamburgers moist.

Hamburger safety:
Cook hamburgers until well done to make sure they are safe to eat. There must be no pink showing. Refrigerate any leftovers right away.

If you would like to have hot dogs (wiener in a bun with onion, ketchup and mustard) instead of hamburgers, you can have:
* *instead of the cheeseburger for the large meal, two hot dogs with no cheese.*
* *instead of a hamburger for the small meal, one hot dog with cheese.*

Use lean or extra-lean ground hamburger when you make hamburgers. One pound of lean hamburger will make three large or four medium cooked hamburger patties. For extra flavor you can mix spices or two teaspoons of dried onion soup into the raw hamburger.

Here are several ways to cook your hamburgers:
* grill on a barbecue
* place them on a rack and broil in the oven
* fry them in a non-stick pan, and soak up the extra fat with a paper towel

Fill your hamburger bun with lots of lettuce, tomato and onion. Add a teaspoon of ketchup, mustard, and relish or cheese spread, if you wish. For the large meal, add one slice of cheese.

Potato Salad

Makes 4 cups of potato salad.

Each 1/2 cup Potato Salad Calories: 86 Carbohydrate: 16 g Protein: 2.3 g Fat: 1.6 g	

4 small cooked potatoes, chopped

1/2 green pepper, finely chopped

2 celery stalks, finely chopped

2 to 3 green onions, finely chopped (or 1 small onion)

5 radishes, sliced

2 tablespoons vinegar

2 tablespoons light mayonnaise

1/2 teaspoon prepared mustard

Salt and pepper, to taste

1 hard boiled egg, chopped

Dash of paprika to sprinkle on top

1. In a big bowl, mix together the potatoes, green pepper, celery, green onions and radishes.
2. In a small bowl, mix together the vinegar, mayonnaise, mustard, salt and pepper. Gently fold in the chopped egg. Pour this into the bowl with the potatoes, and mix gently. Sprinkle the top with paprika.

A nice drink for this meal is light iced tea. There are many kinds that you can buy. You could make your own light iced tea by mixing leftover cold tea with lemon juice and a low-calorie sweetener, to suit your taste.

Watermelon or some other fresh fruit is a great end to this meal.

Potato salad safety:
Once you've made your potato salad, keep it in your refrigerator. As soon as your meal is over, place it back in your refrigerator. Never leave it in the sun.

Check the label of light iced tea packages:
- *Make sure the tea you buy has fewer than 20 calories in a serving.*
- *It will probably say "diet", "calorie-reduced" or "light ("lite") on the label.*

	Per Large Meal	Per Small Meal
Carbohydrates	**81 g**	**73 g**
Protein	**45.0 g**	**30.8 g**
Fat	**27.0 g**	**15.7 g**
Saturated Fat	10.5 g	4.7 g
Cholesterol	145 mg	88 mg
Fiber	7.6 g	6.8 g
Sodium	1550 mg	1192 mg
Vitamin A	138 µg	99 µg
Folic Acid	101 µg	89 µg
Vitamin C	68 mg	60 mg
Potassium	1644 mg	1384 mg
Calcium	283 mg	142 mg
Iron	6.3 mg	5.2 mg

Your Dinner Menu	Large Meal (730 calories)	Small Meal (550 calories)
Cheeseburger / Hamburger with bun and toppings	large burger, with cheese	medium burger
Potato Salad	3/4 cup	1/2 cup
Celery sticks	2 stalks	2 stalks
Dill pickles	2 small, or 1 medium	2 small, or 1 medium
Light iced tea	12 ounces	12 ounces
Watermelon	3 small slices	3 small slices

SMALL MEAL

DINNER 17

Roast Turkey Dinner

Roast turkey is a great meal to have any time of the year. The leftovers come in so handy for sandwiches and other meals. I've made this meal fancier by adding some extras. Even with the extras, the calories in this meal are not any higher than the other meals.

Turkey

- Place your turkey on a rack, breast side up in a covered pan. For the last 15 minutes of cooking, uncover the pan if you wish.
- Cook your turkey for about fifteen minutes per pound in a 350°F oven. Cook to 170°F measured with a thermometer in the inner thigh. Turkey is cooked when the meat moves easily when pierced with a fork.
- Once cooked, remove most of the high-fat skin, and slice the dark and white meat. Dark meat has more fat than white meat.
- Enjoy 1 tablespoon of canned or home-made cranberry sauce on the side.

Potatoes and Gravy

- Use the recipe for Low-Fat Gravy (page 106) and Low-Fat Mashed Potatoes (page 122).

Vegetables

- A lot of vegetables are served with this meal, including carrots, peas, dill pickles, Jellied Vegetable Salad (see recipe on page 139) and asparagus (fresh or canned).

Beverage

In addition to your glass of water, this meal is served with a wine spritzer. A spritzer has fewer calories and alcohol than regular wine. To make a glass of spritzer, add to a glass: 2 ounces (1/4 cup) of dry wine, and fill up the glass with diet ginger ale or diet 7-up.

Dessert

This crustless pumpkin pie is delicious. When I served this to my family, they didn't even miss the crust. It can be served as it is, or with a small amount of a whipped topping.

I leave my turkey unstuffed. Bread stuffing is made with a lot of fat and soaks up more fat from the turkey. If you want to make stuffing—cook it in a greased baking dish (covered) or tin foil. Eat less potato if you also want stuffing.

If you decide to have regular gravy, limit yourself to 1 tablespoon.

If you would prefer to not have alcohol:
- *use non-alcohol wine in the spritzer*
- *drink diet soft drink, sparkling mineral water or soda water*

Crustless Pumpkin Pie

Makes six slices (9-inch glass pie plate).

14 ounce (398 ml) can pumpkin

1/2 cup sugar

1/2 teaspoon salt

1/2 teaspoon ground ginger

1 teaspoon ground cinnamon

1/4 teaspoon ground nutmeg

1/4 teaspoon ground cloves

2 slightly beaten eggs

13 ounce (385 ml) can evaporated skim milk

Each slice of Crustless Pumpkin Pie
Calories: 168
Carbohydrate: 31 g
Protein: 8.1 g
Fat: 2.1 g

*O*ther options for a topping would include whipped cream, packaged mixed toppings or vanilla yogurt. Check the label; whipped topping should have fewer than 20 calories in a 2-tablespoon serving.

*T*his pie is best if made the day before.

1. In a large bowl, mix pumpkin, sugar, salt and spices.
2. Stir in the two slightly beaten eggs and mix well.
3. Add the evaporated skim milk (shake can before opening) and stir until smooth.
4. Pour into a lightly greased glass pie plate (this recipe works best in a glass pie plate instead of metal). Bake in a 400°F oven for about forty minutes, or until knife inserted near the center of the pie comes out clean.

	Per Large Meal	Per Small Meal
Carbohydrates	**108 g**	**83 g**
Protein	**62.3 g**	**43.7 g**
Fat	**8.2 g**	**5.6 g**
Saturated Fat	3.0 g	2.2 g
Cholesterol	214 mg	151 mg
Fiber	10.6 g	9.1 g
Sodium	1199 mg	1061 mg
Vitamin A	1199 µg	1179 µg
Folic Acid	172 µg	163 µg
Vitamin C	73 mg	67 mg
Potassium	1956 mg	1815 mg
Calcium	396 mg	347 mg
Iron	7.0 mg	5.3 mg

Your Dinner Menu	Large Meal (730 calories)	Small Meal (550 calories)
Turkey	3 ounces white meat and 2 ounces of dark meat	3 ounces white meat (or 2 ounces white and 1 ounce dark)
Cranberry sauce	2 teaspoons	2 teaspoons
Low-Fat Mashed Potatoes	1 1/4 cups	3/4 cups
Low-Fat Gravy	4 tablespoons	2 tablespoons
Peas and carrots	1/2 cup	1/2 cup
Asparagus	7 stalks	7 stalks
Dill pickle	1 medium	1 medium
Jellied Vegetable Salad	1/2 cup	1/2 cup
Wine spritzer	1/2 cup	1/2 cup
Crustless Pumpkin Pie	1 slice	1 slice
Whipped topping	2 tablespoons	2 tablespoons

SMALL MEAL

DINNER 18

Baked Macaroni & Cheese

Instead of two eggs, use a small tin of water-packed tuna with the water drained.

Use a low-fat cheese in this recipe and you will be eating less fat.

For extra flavor, add one of these to macaroni and cheese:
- *dash of hot chili sauce*
- *1 tablespoon of salsa*
- *1/4 teaspoon of both oregano and garlic powder*

Baked Macaroni and Cheese

Makes about 5 1/2 cups.

2 cups dry macaroni

2 tablespoons skim milk

2 eggs, beaten with a fork

1/2 a can (5 ounces or 142 ml) tomato soup

1/2 cup loosely packed, shredded Cheddar cheese

2 tablespoons Seasoned Bread Crumbs (see page 131) (optional)

Each 1 cup Baked Macaroni & Cheese
Calories: 241
Carbohydrate: 35 g
Protein: 10.7 g
Fat: 6.4 g

1. Fill a heavy pot with water and bring to a boil. Add the macaroni and boil for ten minutes. Drain.
2. Add the milk, then the eggs, to the macaroni and stir quickly on low heat until the eggs are cooked. Add the tomato soup and cheese and stir some more. It should be ready in two minutes.
3. It is ready to eat now if you want. If you want it baked (as in the picture), place it in a baking dish and sprinkle Seasoned Bread Crumbs on top. Bake in a 375°F oven for half an hour.

Vegetables

- Cut broccoli in pieces and steam or lightly boil. For other low-calorie vegetable choices see page 131.
- Try raw pieces of rutabaga or turnip. For a change, cook turnip with carrots, and mash together once cooked.

For dessert, try this easy and delicious dessert, made with bananas, pineapple, pudding and Graham wafers. It looks as good as it tastes.

Pineapple Surprise

Makes six servings.

| **Each serving Pineapple Surprise** |
| Calories: 148 |
| Carbohydrate: 28 g |
| Protein: 4.0 g |
| Fat: 3.7 g |

1 1/2 cups skim milk

1 package light vanilla instant pudding mix

1 cup frozen whipped topping (regular or light), thawed

8 ounces (227 ml) can crushed pineapple, drained

2 small bananas, sliced thinly

1/4 cup Graham cracker crumbs

(equal to about 4 Graham crackers)

You may want to make Pineapple Surprise with regular pudding instead of light. By doing so, you will add an extra 2 1/2 teaspoons of sugar to each serving.

1. Pour the skim milk into a medium bowl and add the pudding mix.
2. Beat with a whisk or an electric mixer until thickened (about two minutes).
3. Fold in the frozen whipped topping and pineapple until well blended.
4. Add the sliced bananas and Graham cracker crumbs to the pudding mixture. Save some bananas and crumbs for the top. If you want, you can layer the pudding mixture, bananas and crumbs.
5. Put in the fridge until ready to serve.

	Per Large Meal	Per Small Meal
Carbohydrates	**122 g**	**96 g**
Protein	**30.8 g**	**22.8 g**
Fat	**16.9 g**	**12.1 g**
Saturated Fat	8.5 g	6.3 g
Cholesterol	180 mg	112 mg
Fiber	10.3 g	9.4 g
Sodium	1201 mg	986 mg
Vitamin A	321 µg	268 µg
Folic Acid	103 µg	91 µg
Vitamin C	84 mg	84 mg
Potassium	1098 mg	986 mg
Calcium	392 mg	317 mg
Iron	4.4 mg	3.4 mg

Your Dinner Menu	**Large Meal** (730 calories)	**Small Meal** (550 calories)
Baked Macaroni & Cheese	2 cups	1 1/4 cups
Broccoli	1 1/2 cups	1 1/2 cups
Rutabaga or turnip sticks	1/2 cup	1/2 cup
Bread & butter pickles	5 slices	5 slices
Pineapple Surprise	1 serving	1 serving

SMALL MEAL

DINNER 19

Pork Chop & Applesauce

You can place a rack over a pan and broil the meat in the oven. The fat will drip into the pan.

Here are some lower fat cuts of pork:
- *loin or tenderloin*
- *leg, inside round*

Pork does not have to be a rich meal. Trim the fat and barbecue or broil small pork chops. Or cook without fat in a non-stick pan. Pork goes nicely with boiled potatoes sprinkled with fresh or dried parsley.

A small dish of applesauce is served with the pork chop. Instead of applesauce, you could slice an apple and an onion and cook them with the pork.

For another nice change, try a lamb chop with mint sauce, instead of pork chop with applesauce.

This meal is served with an easy-to-make German Bean Salad. This salad will keep in the fridge for a week. This German Bean Salad has a tangy bite; it's not sweet at all. Try making it with a flavored vinegar, as shown in the picture at the side.

German Bean Salad

Makes 4 cups.

4 cups fresh yellow or green beans, cooked, or two 14-ounce (396 ml) cans of cut beans (drained)

1/2 medium onion, thinly sliced

2 tablespoon vinegar

1/4 teaspoon salt (no salt if using canned beans)

1. Cut the beans into 1-inch pieces and place in a salad bowl. If you are using canned beans, drain them and place them in the bowl.
2. Mix with the other ingredients.
3. Leave to stand for thirty minutes. Serve.

Each 1 cup of German Bean Salad
Calories: 33
Carbohydrate: 7 g
Protein: 1.7 g
Fat: 0.2 g

Tapioca pudding is easy to make and healthy. Instead of this pudding you may choose a boxed light pudding, or one of the dessert choices from the other meals, or one cup of milk with a plain cookie.

Tapioca Pudding

Makes four servings.

1 egg (separated)

2 tablespoons sugar

2 cups skim milk

3 tablespoons quick-cooking tapioca

3 tablespoons sugar

Dash of salt

1/2 teaspoon vanilla

**Each serving
Tapioca Pudding**
Calories: 145
Carbohydrate: 28 g
Protein: 5.8 g
Fat: 1.5 g

1. Place the egg white in a bowl and the egg yolk in a small pot. Beat the egg white with a beater until foamy. Gradually add 2 tablespoons of sugar until mixture forms soft peaks.
2. In the pot, beat the yolk with a fork. Add the milk to the yolk. Stir in tapioca, then add 3 tablespoons of sugar and salt.
3. Cook this yolk mixture to a rolling boil, stirring. Take off heat.
4. Pour a small amount of the tapioca mixture over the beaten egg white and blend. Fold the rest of the tapioca mixture into the egg white. Cool on the counter.
5. Stir tapioca after fifteen minutes. Add vanilla and chill.
6. Before serving, put 1 teaspoon of diet jam or a small piece of fruit on top of each serving, if you want.

	Per Large Meal	Per Small Meal
Carbohydrates	**92 g**	**80 g**
Protein	**56.9 g**	**37.6 g**
Fat	**15.1 g**	**9.8 g**
Saturated Fat	5.2 g	3.4 g
Cholesterol	149 mg	112 mg
Fiber	7.9 g	6.8 g
Sodium	604 mg	562 mg
Vitamin A	117 µg	116 µg
Folic Acid	89 µg	77 µg
Vitamin C	45 mg	26 mg
Potassium	2013 mg	1428 mg
Calcium	283 mg	224 mg
Iron	3.4 mg	2.8 mg

Your Dinner Menu	Large Meal (730 calories)	Small Meal (550 calories)
Pork chop	1 medium (5 ounces, cooked)	1 small (3 ounces, cooked)
Applesauce	1/4 cup	1/4 cup
Boiled potatoes with parsley	8 small or 1 large	5 small or 1 medium
German Bean Salad	1 cup	1 cup
Tapioca Pudding	1 serving	1 serving
Coffee	1 cup	1 cup

SMALL MEAL

DINNER 20

Tacos

You can make tacos with a lot or a little spice. You can make tacos using the bean and meat filling below, or using leftover spaghetti sauce, chili con carne or chopped turkey or meat. Tacos are a favorite with my family. Tacos are so easy and kids love to help (even if it does get a bit messy making them; and eating them). For a change, you can make burritos by using a soft flour tortilla shell instead of a hard taco shell.

You could make tacos one day and burritos the next with the rest of the Bean and Meat Filling. If you're cooking for just one or two people, you'll have some extra to freeze.

Canned refried beans have a lot of fat and are not a good choice.

Here are some low-calorie vegetables that taste good in tacos:
- *bean sprouts*
- *chopped tomatoes*
- *chopped green, red or yellow peppers*
- *hot pepper rings (pickled)*
- *shredded lettuce*
- *salsa*

Bean and Meat Filling

Makes 5 cups (enough for twenty tacos).

1 pound lean hamburger

1/3 cup water

1 package taco or burrito spice mix

28 ounce (796 ml) can kidney beans or white beans, including the juice

1. In a medium pot, brown the hamburger. Drain off as much fat as you can.
2. Stir in the water and spice mix. Cook on medium heat for ten minutes. Add extra water if needed. Add the beans and cook for another five minutes.

Tacos

To make each taco you will need:

1 taco shell

1/4 cup Bean and Meat Filling

1 tablespoon shredded cheese

Lots of vegetables

Each Taco
Calories: 175
Carbohydrate: 19 g
Protein: 9.7 g
Fat: 7.7 g

1. Heat the taco shells in the oven at 350° for 5 minutes.
2. Into each hot taco shell put the meat and bean mixture, cheese and vegetables.

Since you eat burritos or tacos with your hands, it's nice to serve other finger foods, too. Try fresh vegetables with this dip.

Vegetable Dip

Makes 1 1/2 cups.

1 cup plain skim milk yogurt	
1/2 cup low-fat sour cream	
2 tablespoons dried onion soup mix	
Chopped green onion tops or parsley	

Each 2 tablespoons Vegetable Dip
Calories: 25
Carbohydrate: 3 g
Protein: 1.5 g
Fat: 0.8 g

1. Mix the first three ingredients together.
2. Put the green onions or parsley on top.

For dessert, make an angel food cake from a mix, or even easier, buy one from a bakery. Angel food cake has the lowest amount of fat of any cake. Serve the angel food cake with fruit, such as strawberries (either fresh or unsweetened frozen), and a dab of frozen or canned whipped topping. Other topping choices are listed on page 159.

	Per Large Meal	Per Small Meal
Carbohydrates	**93 g**	**77 g**
Protein	**35.8 g**	**25.5 g**
Fat	**26.7 g**	**18.0 g**
Saturated Fat	12.8 g	8.8 g
Cholesterol	65 mg	43 mg
Fiber	14.5 g	11.5 g
Sodium	842 mg	628 mg
Vitamin A	264 µg	235 µg
Folic Acid	166 µg	129 µg
Vitamin C	219 mg	218 mg
Potassium	1293 mg	1284 mg
Calcium	325 mg	225 mg
Iron	5.6 mg	4.2 mg

Your Dinner Menu	Large Meal (730 calories)	Small Meal (550 calories)
Bean & Meat Tacos	3	2
Fresh vegetables on the side	2 cups	2 cups
Vegetable Dip	2 tablespoons	2 tablespoons
Angel food cake	3-inch slice	3-inch slice
Strawberries	1/2 cup	1/2 cup
Whipped topping	1 tablespoon	1 tablespoon

SMALL MEAL

DINNER 21

Liver & Onions

Calf liver is the tastiest and most tender, but it costs more than beef liver. Pork liver is a bit stronger tasting than beef liver.

Chicken liver is cheap, tender and tasty. Six chicken livers are equal to about one large serving of beef liver.

You can cook an equal portion of beef kidney as a change from beef liver.

Boil chicken gizzards in a bit of chicken broth for at least an hour until they are tender. About 5 ounces (140 grams) raw chicken gizzards would be an equal portion to the large serving of beef liver.

Iron is needed for healthy blood. Organ meats are one of the best sources of iron. Other good sources of iron include beef, pork and chicken, eggs, oysters, kidney beans, whole-wheat bread, cereals, spinach, dark green lettuce and dried fruit such as raisins.

Do you love liver? Then you'll enjoy this meal. Organ meats such as liver, kidney, gizzards and heart are all rich in iron and other nutrients. But they are also high in cholesterol, so eat small servings, as shown.

Liver and Onions

Makes enough for 3 large or 4 medium servings.

1 medium onion, thinly sliced

1/2 cup beef broth made from 1/2 cup water plus 1 packet (or 1 cube) beef bouillon mix

1/4 cup dry wine or wine vinegar

1 pound (454 grams) beef liver

Each large serving
Calories: 295
Carbohydrate: 15 g
Protein: 37.1 g
Fat: 7.1 g

1. Heat up the beef broth and wine in a non-stick or cast-iron pan. Over low heat, cook the onion slices until soft. Take the onions out of the pan, leaving the liquid.
2. Place the liver in the pan and cook it on high heat for a few minutes on each side. Make sure it is cooked through but not overcooked. Overcooking makes liver tough. Just before serving, return the onions to the pan to warm them up.
3. At the table, pour the broth from the pan over your liver and rice, if desired.

Liver is also easy and tasty cooked on the barbecue. On a hot barbecue the liver will cook quickly—be careful it doesn't overcook.

For your starch, you may have rice, as shown, or potatoes.

The vegetables for this meal are carrots and tomatoes. Choose either canned tomatoes or fresh sliced tomatoes.

For dessert there is fruit salad served with two small vanilla wafers (or one plain cookie, such as an Arrowroot biscuit). To make your fruit salad, mix together any of your favorite fresh or frozen fruits.

	Per Large Meal	Per Small Meal
Carbohydrates	**109 g**	**92 g**
Protein	**45.9 g**	**31.3 g**
Fat	**10.4 g**	**7.6 g**
Saturated Fat	3.4 g	2.4 g
Cholesterol	645 mg	410 mg
Fiber	10.5 g	10.1 g
Sodium	1145 mg	897 mg
Vitamin A	18,118 µg	11,841 µg
Folic Acid	404 µg	276 µg
Vitamin C	77 mg	66 mg
Potassium	1729 mg	1487 mg
Calcium	159 mg	143 mg
Iron	14.9 mg	10.4 mg

Your Dinner Menu	**Large Meal** (730 calories)	**Small Meal** (550 calories)
Liver	2 slices (large serving)	1 slice (medium serving)
Cooked sliced onions	1/2 cup	1/2 cup
Rice	1 cup	3/4 cup
Carrots	1/2 cup	1/2 cup
Canned tomatoes	1 cup	1 cup
Fresh fruit salad	1 cup	1 cup
Vanilla wafers	2 small	2 small

SMALL MEAL

DINNER 22

Sun Burger

These meatless burgers are delicious when served on a bagel or hamburger bun. Add to your bagel: lots of vegetables, such as lettuce, tomatoes, onions and cucumbers.

Sun Burgers

Makes 12 burgers.

1 1/2 cups cooked rice, brown or white

19 ounce (540 ml) can romano beans (or other beans, such as pinto or kidney)

1/3 cup sesame seeds

1/3 cup sunflower seeds

2 tablespoons wheat germ

1/4 teaspoon basil

1/4 teaspoon pepper

1/2 teaspoon garlic powder

1 teaspoon parsley flakes

1 teaspoon of dried dill weed

1 egg

1 cup loosely packed, shredded mozzarella cheese

Each Sun Burger
Calories: 153
Carbohydrate: 17 g
Protein: 8.5 g
Fat: 6.3 g

Using a low-fat cheese will reduce the fat.

1. Cook rice or use cold rice from the night before.
2. Drain the beans. Put them in a small bowl and mash them with a fork or a masher.
3. In a large bowl, mix all the ingredients. Mix with a large spoon or fork, or use your hands.
4. Form mixture into patties. Cook until nicely browned in a non-stick frying pan or heavy frying pan (lightly greased).

Kale and Orange Salad

This salad is made with kale leaves, and slices of bok choy, broccoli, oranges and strawberries. This salad is rich in calcium, iron and vitamin C. Remove the tough stem of the kale and chop the leaves in fine strips. Try adding some purslane greens (see page 18). Use your favorite salad dressing, and try a sprinkle of sesame seeds, ground flax or walnuts on top.

This dessert is easy to make and has a nice light flavor.

Dream Delight

Makes four 1-cup servings.

1 package unflavored gelatin

1 package light gelatin, raspberry or any other flavor

1 package dessert topping mix (enough to make 2 cups)

1 1/4 cups boiling water

1 1/4 cups cold water

Each serving Dream Delight
Calories: 76
Carbohydrate: 6 g
Protein: 3.4 g
Fat: 4.3 g

You may want to make this dessert with regular gelatin instead of light. By doing so, you will add an extra 4 teaspoons of sugar to each serving.

1. Place the light gelatin and the unflavored gelatin in a bowl.
2. Add 1 1/4 cups boiling water. Stir until the gelatin is mixed in. Then add 1 1/4 cups cold water and stir. Refrigerate.
3. Remove the gelatin from the fridge after about forty-five minutes. It should be as thick as an unbeaten egg white. Do not allow the gelatin to get too firm.
4. Mix the dry whipped topping mix as shown on the box.
5. Blend topping with a beater into gelatin mixture until well mixed.
6. Pour into four dessert bowls. Refrigerate to set.

	Per Large Meal	Per Small Meal
Carbohydrates	**106 g**	**89 g**
Protein	**33.7 g**	**24.2 g**
Fat	**22.1 g**	**14.0 g**
Saturated Fat	8.0 g	6.2 g
Cholesterol	70 mg	47 mg
Fiber	11.3 g	8.0 g
Sodium	1270 mg	1132 mg
Vitamin A	343 µg	299 µg
Folic Acid	266 µg	199 µg
Vitamin C	138 mg	138 mg
Potassium	1041 mg	845 mg
Calcium	419 mg	292 mg
Iron	7.5 mg	5.8 mg

Your Dinner Menu	**Large Meal** (730 calories)	**Small Meal** (550 calories)
Sun Burgers	2	1
Bagel	1	1
Light mayonnaise	2 teaspoons	1/2 teaspoon
Kale and Orange Salad	large	large
Oil-free salad dressing	1 tablespoon	1 tablespoon
Dream Delight	1 cup	1 cup

SMALL MEAL

DINNER 23

Salmon & Potato Dish

This is one of the meals that my husband likes to make. It is easy and is always popular. It can be made with canned salmon or tuna, or any kind of leftover fish.

*Add one of these to
your salmon for some
extra flavor:*
- *1/2 teaspoon
horseradish*
- *1/4 teaspoon
mustard*
- *1 tablespoon salsa*
- *1 tablespoon
spaghetti sauce*

- *Seasoned Bread
Crumbs (page 130)
or Parmesan cheese
can be sprinkled on
top of this dish.*

- *Instant mashed
potatoes can be used.
They are softer and
moister than fresh
mashed potatoes.*

Salmon and Potato Dish

Makes one small baking dish (2 large or 3 small servings).

Each large serving
Calories: 518
Carbohydrate: 34 g
Protein: 34.9 g
Fat: 26.8 g

1 can (213 g) of pink salmon

(canned in water)

Dash of pepper

2 cups mashed potato (leftover or fresh)

1 cup loosely packed, shredded Cheddar cheese

1. Drain the water from the salmon can. Mash the salmon with bones. Put the salmon on the bottom of a small baking dish. Sprinkle with pepper and half the shredded cheese.
2. Spread the mashed potato on top of the salmon and cheese.
3. Sprinkle the rest of the cheese on top.
4. Bake in a 350°F oven for half an hour, or microwave for eight minutes.

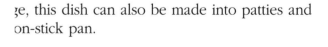
ge, this dish can also be made into patties and on-stick pan.

Corn is the sweet vegetable with this meal, and spinach and tomato juice are the low-calorie vegetables.

You can buy spinach fresh or frozen.

Choose either 1/3 cup of creamed corn or 1/2 cup of kernel corn for your vegetable. Creamed corn has sugar added, so a smaller serving is enough.

The dessert is light gelatin with fruit.

Spinach is rich in iron and folic acid.

Instead of fruit cocktail, you can use a can of other fruit such as peaches. Chop the fruit into pieces.

If you want, you can use 1 3/4 cups of fresh chopped fruit instead of canned fruit. When you use fresh fruit, add 1 cup of cold water instead of 1/4 cup.

Light Gelatin with Fruit

Makes three 1-cup servings.

1 package light gelatin
1 cup boiling water
1/4 cup cold water
14-ounce (398 ml) can fruit cocktail, with juice

Each 1 cup Light Gelatin
Calories: 75
Carbohydrate: 17 g
Protein: 2.4 g
Fat: 0 g

1. Put the gelatin in a medium bowl (not plastic).
2. Add the boiling water. Stir until gelatin is all mixed in.
3. Add the cold water and fruit cocktail and stir.
4. Pour into three dessert bowls. Refrigerate to set.

	Per Large Meal	Per Small Meal
Carbohydrates	**87 g**	**70 g**
Protein	**45.0 g**	**32.6 g**
Fat	**27.2 g**	**18.4 g**
Saturated Fat	13.7 g	9.2 g
Cholesterol	84 mg	56 mg
Fiber	10.5 g	9.7 g
Sodium	1441 mg	1218 mg
Vitamin A	615 µg	556 µg
Folic Acid	192 µg	189 µg
Vitamin C	38 mg	38 mg
Potassium	1772 mg	1595 mg
Calcium	809 mg	619 mg
Iron	4.9 mg	4.3 mg

Your Dinner Menu	**Large Meal** (730 calories)	**Small Meal** (550 calories)
Salmon & Potato Dish	1/2 the recipe	1/3 the recipe
Corn	3/4 cup	1/2 cup
Spinach	1/2 cup	1/2 cup
Tomato juice	1/2 cup	1/2 cup
Celery	1/4 stalk (in tomato juice)	1 1/4 stalks
Light Gelatin with Fruit	1 cup	1 cup

SMALL MEAL

Hamburger Noodle Dish

Most packages of noodles and sauce mix that can be added to help hamburger are high in fat. This recipe is lower in fat.

Hamburger Noodle Dish

Makes 7 1/3 cups (about 4 large or 6 small servings).

Each 1 cup Hamburger Noodle Dish
Calories: 281
Carbohydrate: 37 g
Protein: 17.8 g
Fat: 6.6 g

1 pound lean hamburger

1 large onion, chopped

1/4 teaspoon pepper

10 ounce (284 ml) can tomato soup

10 ounce (284 ml) can mushroom pieces (drained)

1 cup skim milk

1 teaspoon Worcestershire sauce

4 cups dry corkscrew noodles (or 2 1/2 cups macaroni)

1. In a large heavy pan, brown the hamburger. Drain off the fat.
2. Add the chopped onion to the hamburger and cook until the onions are soft. Add water if too dry. Add all other ingredients except the noodles. Cook for fifteen minutes.
3. While the hamburger and onions are cooking, add the noodles to a pot of boiling water. Drain the cooked noodles.
4. Add cooked noodles to the hamburger mixture. Cook for five more minutes.

The mushrooms add a nice flavor to this recipe.

If you want a bit more zip, you can always add a dash of hot pepper sauce.

The corkscrew noodles look nice in this dish, but if you don't have them, use macaroni.

This meal is served with mixed vegetables and steamed cabbage. You may drizzle 1 tablespoon of light cheese spread on your cabbage, instead of the butter or margarine.

For dessert, have a piece of fresh fruit.

"Healthy meals and snacks give me the energy I need to do my work."

	Per Large Meal	Per Small Meal
Carbohydrates	**113 g**	**89 g**
Protein	**38.1 g**	**27.9 g**
Fat	**16.3 g**	**10.8 g**
Saturated Fat	5.1 g	3.4 g
Cholesterol	55 mg	39 mg
Fiber	13.7 g	11.1 g
Sodium	893 mg	634 mg
Vitamin A	470 µg	336 µg
Folic Acid	97 µg	80 µg
Vitamin C	50 mg	47 mg
Potassium	1440 mg	1189 mg
Calcium	211 mg	171 mg
Iron	6.3 mg	4.8 mg

Your Dinner Menu	**Large Meal** (730 calories)	**Small Meal** (550 calories)
Hamburger Noodle Dish	1 3/4 cups	1 1/4 cups
Mixed vegetables	1 cup	3/4 cup
Cabbage	1 cup	1 cup
Margarine or butter	1 teaspoon	1/2 teaspoon
Grapes	1 1/4 cups (33 grapes)	1 1/4 cups (33 grapes)

SMALL MEAL

DINNER 25

Pizza

This meal can be eaten out in a restaurant or you can make the meal at home using the recipe below. The photograph shows a thick crust pizza. You may want to choose a thin crust pizza which will have less calories. Choose a pizza with lots of vegetables and don't go heavy on the meat and cheese.

If you are making your own pizza at home, you can make it lower in fat by using lean meat and low-fat cheese, and lots of vegetables of your choice. Try this easy recipe.

Pizza Sauce:
Mix one 14 ounce (398 ml) can of tomato sauce with 1/2 teaspoon oregano and 1/2 teaspoon garlic powder.

For extra flavor, add in:
- *1 small onion (finely chopped)*
- *1 clove chopped garlic (instead of powder)*
- *1/2 stalk chopped celery*
- *pinch of cinnamon and cloves*

Homemade Pizza

Makes one 12-inch pizza (8 medium slices).

Pizza shell (ready-made, 12-inch)

1 cup Pizza Sauce (see side bar)

Per medium slice
Calories: 298
Carbohydrate: 40 g
Protein: 11.5 g
Fat: 10.5 g

Vegetables, such as mushrooms, peppers, onions, tomatoes, broccoli, zucchini, or eggplant

1/2 cup pineapple chunks

2 ounces of sliced ham, sausage or pepperoni

3/4 cup loosely packed low-fat shredded cheese

1. Spread the pizza sauce on the pizza shell.
2. Add the vegetables, pineapple and meat. Top with cheese.
3. Place on your oven rack or use a pizza pan, if you have one. Bake in a 350°F oven for fifteen minutes, until the cheese bubbles.

You can make mini pizzas on opened hamburger buns or on English muffins or pita shells.

Have a salad with your pizza. With your meal enjoy a diet soft drink (as shown) or a small glass of tomato juice. Also have water to drink.

Have a fruit for dessert.

A few restaurant tips:

- Eat a fruit or a fresh vegetable snack before you go to a restaurant so you won't be so hungry and overeat.
- It may help if you decide what you'll order before you go. Or better still, decide what you won't order.
- Start with a salad, clear soup or vegetable soup. Even fast food restaurants now have salads.
- Ask for low-fat salad dressings on the side.
- Don't be shy about asking for foods to be made to your liking. For example, if you order a sandwich, ask for it to be unbuttered.
- If your meal is bigger than your portions should be, ask the waiter to package your leftovers, so you can take them home.

*Drinking regular soft drinks, sweetened beverages, and even juices, will give you extra sugar you don't need. Remember, water is what your body needs when you are thirsty (see page 25). For more information about sugar in beverages, go to **mealsforgoodhealth.com** (Newsletters and Resources).*

	Per Large Meal	Per Small Meal
Carbohydrates	**106 g**	**80 g**
Protein	**26.8 g**	**19.2 g**
Fat	**25.7 g**	**18.7 g**
Saturated Fat	5.0 g	3.5 g
Cholesterol	21 mg	14 mg
Fiber	11.2 g	8.7 g
Sodium	1455 mg	1056 mg
Vitamin A	184 µg	163 µg
Folic Acid	245 µg	198 µg
Vitamin C	29 mg	25 mg
Potassium	1346 mg	1122 mg
Calcium	286 mg	214 mg
Iron	6.1 mg	4.3 mg

Your Dinner Menu	**Large Meal** (730 calories)	**Small Meal** (550 calories)
12-inch Pizza	2 medium slices	1 large slice
Salad	large	large
Oil-free salad dressing	1 tablespoon	1 tablespoon
Diet soft drink	large	large
Nectarine	1	1

SMALL MEAL

DINNER 26

Grilled Chicken Bun & Fries

Yes, you may still eat out at fast food restaurants—occasionally. Most foods in restaurants are high in fat.

Since fries are the most common food ordered in restaurants, they are included in this meal; but choose a small order.

If you decide to make this meal at home, make Baked Low-Fat Fries (page 138), baked frozen french fries or a baked potato.

Instead of a grilled chicken breast on a bun (as shown in the photograph), you could order:
- a small serving of six chicken nuggets with sauce
- a single fish burger
- a cheeseburger

Hot Chicken Salad & Biscuits:
Turn frozen breaded chicken strips into a fast meal at home by making a chicken salad meal. Visit *mealsforgoodhealth.com* for the recipe and full meal menu.

Salad with a light dressing is included with this meal. No salad dressing is included with the small meal due to the calories (see side bar). In a restaurant, the best choice is to have your salad plain or with half a package of "light" vinegar-based dressing (vinaigrette).

Since this meal is higher in fat than other meals, a dessert is not included with the small meal.

Have water and a diet soft drink, if you like.

Try to enjoy your coffee or tea with no milk or sugar, or less of both.

Salad dressings:
- *Some of the "light" salad dressings in restaurants are still high in calories. They can have up to 60 calories in one package. Check the label.*

- *The regular salad dressings in restaurants may have 200 calories in one package.*

	Per Large Meal	Per Small Meal
Carbohydrates	**89 g**	**63 g**
Protein	**29.1 g**	**25.1 g**
Fat	**38.2 g**	**31.1 g**
Saturated Fat	9.8 g	8.8 g
Cholesterol	102 mg	99 mg
Fiber	5.3 g	3.8 g
Sodium	1345 mg	1097 mg
Other nutrients not available.		

Your Dinner Menu	**Large Meal** (730 calories)	**Small Meal** (550 calories)
Grilled chicken on a bun	1	1
French fries	1 small order	1 small order
Ketchup	1 tablespoon	1 tablespoon
Salad	1 small	1 small
Light vinaigrette salad dressing	1 package	–
Diet soft drink	large	large
Yogurt cone	1 small	–

195

SMALL MEAL

DINNER 27

Chinese Stir Fry

Put your rice on to cook before you start making the Stir Fry.

Other protein choices:
Instead of raw meat, chicken, or fish, you could use:
- *5 ounces of leftover cooked chicken, meat or fish*
- *7 ounces of shrimp (23 jumbo shrimp)*
- *1/2 cup firm tofu (cut in chunks)*
- *28 almonds.*

W*ash your knife and cutting board with hot soapy water if you use raw chicken or raw meat.*

I*f you are making Chinese food at home, use little or no fat in a pot, or a non-stick pan or wok. Your pan has to be large enough to hold all the vegetables.*

Chinese Stir Fry

Makes 4 cups (2 large meal servings).

Each 1 cup
Calories: 122
Carbohydrate: 16 g
Protein: 11.5 g
Fat: 2.4 g

3/4 cup (or 6 ounces) raw lean red meat, chicken or fish (thinly sliced)

1 packet chicken or beef bouillon mix

2 tablespoons water

1 small onion

1 to 2 cloves chopped garlic

4 to 6 cups loosely packed vegetable pieces

2 teaspoons cornstarch

1/4 cup cold water

1 tablespoon soy sauce

1/4 teaspoon ginger powder

1. Chop up or slice your onion, garlic and 4 cups of vegetables. I usually put in one bowl the vegetables that need the most cooking, such as carrots and broccoli. In a second bowl I put the vegetables that need less cooking, such as bean sprouts. Put the bowls of vegetables to the side.
2. Place the raw meat (or other protein choice) in your cold wok or frying pan. Sprinkle the bouillon mix on your meat and stir. Add 2 tablespoons of water. Heat up your wok or frying pan and cook for about three minutes. If you are using cooked leftover meat instead of raw meat, it doesn't need to be cooked first.
3. Add the onions, garlic and first bowl of vegetables. Stir at high heat for five to ten minutes until cooked. Now add the second bowl of vegetables.
4. In a small bowl, mix together the cornstarch, 1/4 cup of cold water, soy sauce and ginger. Add this to your wok. Cook for another minute or two.

Fresh vegetables are best in a stir-fry, but you could also use frozen or canned vegetables. Try any of these vegetables:

- bamboo shoots (canned)
- bean sprouts
- broccoli (pieces)
- cabbage (shredded)
- carrots or celery (sliced)
- cauliflower (pieces)
- baby corn (canned)
- mushrooms (sliced)
- green onions (chopped)
- frozen peas or whole fresh snow peas
- green pepper (strips)

This meal includes beef broth and soda crackers. You can order this first when you are eating at a Chinese restaurant.

Fill up on the low-calorie vegetable dishes. You may add a bit of soy sauce to your rice if you wish. Fried rice is high in fat. In a restaurant just mix in a bit of fried rice with your white rice, if you wish.

Stay away from deep-fried, battered foods and foods in sweet sauces.

For dessert, a fortune cookie is a good low-calorie choice. Good luck!

	Per Large Meal	Per Small Meal
Carbohydrates	**132 g**	**103 g**
Protein	**38.4 g**	**30.6 g**
Fat	**7.1 g**	**5.7 g**
Saturated Fat	2.1 g	1.7 g
Cholesterol	38 mg	29 mg
Fiber	12.1 g	10.2 g
Sodium	2887 mg	2538 mg
Vitamin A	635 µg	514 µg
Folic Acid	134 µg	106 µg
Vitamin C	97 mg	75 mg
Potassium	1753 mg	1464 mg
Calcium	456 mg	418 mg
Iron	4.6 mg	3.5 mg

Your Dinner Menu	**Large Meal** (730 calories)	**Small Meal** (550 calories)
Beef broth	1 cup	1 cup
Chinese Stir Fry	2 cups	1 1/2 cups
White rice	1 1/4 cups	3/4 cup
Skim or 1 percent milk	1 cup	1 cup
Pear	1	1
Fortune cookies	2	2

SOLUTIONS WILL COME TO YOU
WHILE YOU ARE WALKING.

SMALL MEAL

DINNER 28

Denver Sandwich & Soup

A sandwich and soup is a light choice for dinner in a restaurant. The sandwich could be a Denver, a club house or a bacon, lettuce and tomato sandwich. Ask for your bread or toast without butter or mayonnaise, or ask the waiter to "go light" on the butter or mayonnaise. Also ask the waiter to hold the French fries. If you want to make a Denver sandwich at home, here's the recipe.

Denver Sandwich

Makes one sandwich.

Each Sandwich
Calories: 358
Carbohydrate: 29 g
Protein: 19.6 g
Fat: 18.2 g

1 slice (1 ounce) bacon or ham

2 eggs

1 tablespoon chopped parsley, green onion tops, onion or chives

Pepper to taste

2 slices toast, each spread with 1/2 teaspoon butter, margarine or mayonnaise (1 teaspoon if light)

Lettuce

1. Chop the bacon and cook. Drain all fat and soak up extra fat with a paper towel. If you are using chopped ham instead of bacon, you don't need to cook it first.
2. In a small bowl, beat the eggs with a fork. Add the bacon or ham and the parsley or onion tops.
3. Cook in a non-stick pan free of fat. Stir on and off.
4. Place egg mix on piece of toast.
5. Add lettuce or other vegetables to the sandwich.

If you don't care for tomato soup, have vegetable soup or a glass of tomato juice instead. Mushroom and green pea soup have the most calories of all the cream soups. Choose these less often.

These cracker servings have about the same calories:
- 1 bread stick
- 2 soda crackers
- 1 snackbread cracker
- 2 melba toast
- 1 ritz-like party cracker

There is no dessert with this meal. If you would like to have a small fruit, then omit the bread sticks. Or choose a very low-calorie dessert such as light gelatin or a bought sugar-free popsicle.

	Per Large Meal	Per Small Meal
Carbohydrates	**76 g**	**61 g**
Protein	**34.5 g**	**24.7 g**
Fat	**33.4 g**	**24.3 g**
Saturated Fat	8.6 g	6.0 g
Cholesterol	653 mg	436 mg
Fiber	12.0 g	8.8 g
Sodium	2366 mg	2001 mg
Vitamin A	494 µg	369 µg
Folic Acid	225 µg	188 µg
Vitamin C	19 mg	17 mg
Potassium	1132 mg	964 mg
Calcium	226 mg	173 mg
Iron	7.7 mg	5.9 mg

Your Dinner Menu	**Large Meal** (730 calories)	**Small Meal** (550 calories)
Tomato soup (made with water)	1 cup	1 cup
Bread sticks	1 1/2	1 1/2
Denver Sandwich	1 1/2 sandwiches	1 sandwich
Salad	large	large
Oil-free salad dressing	1 tablespoon	1 tablespoon

SMALL MEAL

DINNER *29*

Shish Kebobs

> **A** *true Greek shish kebob is called souvlaki and is made only with meat. It would usually be soaked in olive oil, so would be high in calories.*

Shish kebobs can be one of the lowest fat meal choices in a Greek or Middle Eastern restaurant. Try this delicious low-fat marinade for your meat, or simply baste your meat with your favorite barbecue sauce.

Shish Kebob Marinade

Makes enough for two shish kebobs.

2 tablespoons soy sauce

2 tablespoons finely chopped onion

1 clove garlic, crushed or finely chopped
   (or 1/2 teaspoon garlic powder)

1 tablespoon minced ginger root
   (or 1 teaspoon ginger powder)

2 tablespoons dry wine (or wine vinegar)

Each tablespoon of Marinade
Calories: 22
Carbohydrate: 5 g
Protein: 0.8 g
Fat: 0.1 g

Mix the marinade ingredients together in a dish. Place the meat in the marinade and let it sit in the fridge for a couple of hours.

Shish Kebobs

To make each shish kebob you will need:
Meat (1 1/2-inch cubes of lean lamb or beef)
For large meal: 4 cubes (6 ounces, raw)
For small meal: 3 cubes (4 ounces, raw)
Vegetables
Cherry tomatoes, whole fresh mushrooms, cubes of green pepper, whole small onions (or chunks of onion), zucchini, eggplant, or any other vegetables you like.

1. Put the meat and vegetables on skewers, as shown in the picture. Brush with the marinade. If you want your meat well done, broil or barbecue it for five minutes before adding the vegetables.
2. Broil or barbecue for five to ten minutes or until cooked.

For a change, you can add 1 tablespoon of tomato sauce (or pizza sauce, see page 190) to your cooked rice.

This Greek Salad includes tomatoes, onions, green pepper, feta cheese and black olives. Feel free to add lettuce also. Traditional Greek salad also has lots of olive oil. This recipe is an oil-free variety. If you would like to add 2 tablespoons olive oil instead of the oil free dressing*, cut your meat cubes back to 1" cubes to allow for the extra calories.

If you are having this meal in a restaurant, remember to ask for light salad dressing on the side.

Greek Salad

Makes two large salads.

2 large tomatoes, cut in wedges

1/2 medium onion, sliced

1/2 green pepper, in chunks

1/2 small cucumber

1/4 cup feta cheese, crumbled or chunks

4 black olives

2 tablespoons oil-free Italian dressing (or olive oil*)

Sprinkle of oregano

Each large Greek Salad
Calories: 151
Carbohydrate: 13 g
Protein: 6.2 g
Fat: 9.4 g

1. Mix together the tomatoes, onions, green pepper, cucumber, feta cheese and olives.
2. Before serving, add salad dressing and sprinkle with oregano.

This meal ends with a low-fat dessert: apple sprinkled with a touch of cinnamon and icing sugar. Instead of apple, you could have an orange or 1/2 cup of cantaloupe, melon or grapes.

	Per Large Meal	Per Small Meal
Carbohydrates	87 g	69 g
Protein	42.0 g	32.2 g
Fat	24.5 g	17.3 g
Saturated Fat	9.5 g	7.7 g
Cholesterol	95 mg	78 mg
Fiber	7.2 g	6.6 g
Sodium	1863 mg	1608 mg
Vitamin A	205 µg	105 µg
Folic Acid	89 µg	76 µg
Vitamin C	104 mg	84 mg
Potassium	1249 mg	1099 mg
Calcium	272 mg	255 mg
Iron	7.2 mg	5.6 mg

Your Dinner Menu	Large Meal (730 calories)	Small Meal (550 calories)
Shish Kebob	1 made with 4 cubes of beef	1 made with 3 cubes of beef
Rice	3/4 cup	3/4 cup
Greek Salad with dressing	1 large	1 large
Crusty white bun	1	–
Margarine	1 teaspoon	–
Cinnamon apple rings	1/2 3-inch apple with 1/2 teaspoon icing sugar plus cinnamon	1/2 3-inch apple with 1/2 teaspoon icing sugar plus cinnamon

SMALL MEAL

DINNER 30

Roti with Curried Filling

Rotis and chapatis are flat East Indian breads made from flour and water. Two chapatis would equal 1 roti shell. Rotis or chapatis can be bought ready-made.

If you can't find rotis or chapatis, you can put the filling in 2 pita shells or 2 flour tortillas. 1 1/2 cups of rice could also replace a roti shell.

In the Caribbean, rotis are served folded around a filling of curried meat, chicken or beans and potatoes. Sometimes the rotis are eaten on the side with a curried dish.

Here are two ways to serve your cucumbers:
Slice them thinly and put in a bowl with either:
1. plain low-fat yogurt, flavored with mint or a sprinkle of paprika,
2. vinegar, lemon juice or lime juice

Curried Chick Peas and Potato Filling

Makes 3 cups (enough for six rotis).

Each Roti
Calories: 512
Carbohydrate: 95 g
Protein: 13.6 g
Fat: 8.7 g

1/4 cup water

1 teaspoon vegetable oil

1 medium onion, chopped

2 garlic cloves, finely chopped or crushed

1 tablespoon curry powder (mild or hot)

Dash of hot sauce or chili powder

2 small potatoes, cooked and chopped in small chunks

19 ounce (540 ml) can chick peas, including juice

1. Heat the water and oil in a heavy pot and add the onions, garlic, curry powder and hot sauce. Cook at low heat until the onions are soft.
2. Add the cooked potatoes and canned chickpeas with juice and cook for half an hour. Cool and put in the fridge overnight.

Making the Rotis

The next day, re-heat the Filling and place 1/2 cup in the middle of each roti. Fold one side over the mixture, then the other. Fold ends toward the center to make a neat package. Turn it over on the plate so the folds are underneath. Microwave on high for three to four minutes, or heat in a hot oven for half an hour.

This meal is served with carrot sticks and cucumbers. The large meal also has plantains. Plantains look like large green bananas (see photograph). But unlike a banana, plantains need to be cooked before eating. Plantain is ready to use when the skin has turned partly black on the outside. Then you can peel it, cut it in strips and boil it until soft. Next, lightly brush it with margarine and roast or broil it in the oven. It can also be boiled, then fried in a non-stick pan. It is served as a starchy vegetable (like corn or potatoes).

The dessert for this meal is coconut meringues, which are made with sugar, but no fat—so the calories of this dessert are low. Two of these meringues have about the same amount of sugar and calories as a small piece of fruit.

Coconut Meringues

Makes twenty-eight 2-inch meringues.

Each Coconut Meringue
Calories: 31
Carbohydrate: 7 g
Protein: 0.5 g
Fat: 0.1 g

1 cup sugar

1/4 tsp cream of tartar

4 egg whites, at room temperature (throw out the yolks)

1/2 teaspoon coconut flavoring

1 tablespoon unsweetened coconut (optional)

1. In a small bowl, mix the sugar with the cream of tartar.
2. Beat the egg whites until stiff. Add the sugar and cream of tartar mixture slowly and continue beating until the mixture forms stiff peaks. Beat in the coconut flavoring.
3. Drop heaping tablespoonfuls onto two ungreased cookie sheets. Sprinkle the coconut on top of the meringues. Bake at 200°F for two hours. After 1 1/2 hours, check to see if they are ready. They should be dry when you poke them with a skewer or toothpick. When they're ready, turn the oven off and let them sit in the oven for another two hours.
4. Once cooled, store in a cookie jar or plastic container.

	Per Large Meal	Per Small Meal
Carbohydrates	**144 g**	**107 g**
Protein	**18.0 g**	**14.9 g**
Fat	**11.0 g**	**8.9 g**
Saturated Fat	2.0 g	1.7 g
Cholesterol	1 mg	0 mg
Fiber	11.2 g	8.6 g
Sodium	716 mg	652 mg
Vitamin A	912 µg	289 µg
Folic Acid	118 µg	93 µg
Vitamin C	30 mg	12 mg
Potassium	1280 mg	706 mg
Calcium	167 mg	110 mg
Iron	3.9 mg	3.2 mg

Your Dinner Menu	**Large Meal** (730 calories)	**Small Meal** (550 calories)
Bean & Potato Roti	1 roti	1 roti
Roasted plantain (brushed lightly with 1/2 teaspoon of margarine)	1/2	—
Carrot sticks	1 medium carrot	1/3 medium carrot
Cucumbers (in yogurt)	1/2 medium cucumber plus 2 tablespoons of yogurt	1/2 medium cucumber
Coconut Meringues	2	1

SMALL MEAL

DINNER 31

Tandoori Chicken & Rice

This recipe is also delicious when made with curry powder instead of the tandoori mix. If you use curry powder, the sauce will be a golden curry color. The tandoori mix will make the sauce reddish.

It is important to boil the sauce for five minutes. Raw chicken has a lot of bacteria, and boiling will make the sauce safe to eat.

Tandoori chicken can be served with either:
*   *rice, as shown in the photograph (my favorite is Basmati rice)*
*   *naan bread*
*   *chapati, an East Indian flat bread similar to roti.*

I fell in love with tandoori chicken when I lived in Kenya. This delicious meal is spicy but not hot. The chicken is coated in a tasty low-fat coating and then broiled or barbecued. The tandoori chicken is eaten with rice or naan bread. Look for naan bread at your grocery store, or make it at home using the delicious recipe found at ***mealsforgoodhealth.com***

Tandoori Chicken and Sauce

Makes 5 large or 8 small servings.

Sauce:

	Each large serving
	Calories: 286
	Carbohydrate: 8 g
	Protein: 41.6 g
	Fat: 8.9 g

1 1/2 cups plain (white) skim milk yogurt

1 1/2 tablespoons store-bought tandoori spice mix

1 1/2 tablespoons vinegar

1 1/2 tablespoons lemon juice

2 1/2 lbs (1 kg) of chicken, cut in pieces with the skin taken off.

1. In a large bowl or pot, mix all the ingredients for the sauce.
2. Make some small cuts in each chicken piece so the yogurt sauce can flavor the meat. Add the chicken to the bowl or pot, making sure that it is covered with sauce. Cover and place in the fridge for at least four hours, or overnight.
3. Gently shake any extra sauce from the chicken and barbecue or place on a rack in a pan and grill in the oven (about 5 inches from the grill). Cook for ten to fifteen minutes on each side until well done.
4. Put the leftover sauce in a small heavy pan and boil for 5 minutes. Give each person a small dish of this sauce for dunking their chicken and putting on their rice.

A nice finish to this meal is a small piece of tropical fruit, such as mango or papaya.

Serve this meal with chai tea made with an equal part of hot skim milk, and if you want, 1 teaspoon of sugar, honey or low-calorie sweetener.

Poppadums:
If you've never had poppadums, you don't know what you're missing! They can be bought in large food stores and in specialty food stores. They are 5-7 inches round and come in mild or hot (spicy). All you need to do is place them under a hot broiler and in one or two minutes they will bubble and turn a golden brown. Broil both sides. Or run them quickly under tap water to wet them and then pop them in the microwave at high power for about forty seconds. These crunchy treats are great with a curry meal or can be eaten as a snack.

	Per Large Meal	Per Small Meal
Carbohydrates	**105 g**	**87 g**
Protein	**55.9 g**	**38.0 g**
Fat	**10.3 g**	**6.6 g**
Saturated Fat	2.5 g	1.7 g
Cholesterol	156 mg	95 mg
Fiber	5.5 g	5.3 g
Sodium	825 mg	742 mg
Vitamin A	336 µg	319 µg
Folic Acid	59 µg	50 µg
Vitamin C	55 mg	52 mg
Potassium	1275 mg	1025 mg
Calcium	412 mg	346 mg
Iron	4.4 mg	3.2 mg

Your Dinner Menu	**Large Meal** (730 calories)	**Small Meal** (550 calories)
Tandoori Chicken	1 large leg	1 small leg
Tandoori Sauce	4 tablespoons	2 tablespoons
Rice (Basmati)	1 cup	3/4 cup
Bed of lettuce with tomato and cucumber	1/2 medium tomato and sliced cucumber	1/2 medium tomato and sliced cucumber
Poppadums	2	2
Mango	1/2	1/2
Chai tea made with milk	1 cup	1 cup

SMALL MEAL

Snacks

Snacks

In this section you will find photographs of four groups of snacks. The groups are low-calorie snacks, small snacks, medium snacks and large snacks. The calories for each snack within each group are about the same. The number of snacks you choose will depend on how many calories a day you want. Look at the chart on page 9 that shows the calories of the small and large meals, and different snacks.

For most of us it's good to choose no more than three of the small, medium or large snacks a day.

Three small snacks add up to 150 calories, three medium snacks add up to 300 calories and three large snacks add up to 600 calories.

Low-calorie snacks:

- These snacks have just 20 calories or less. These foods are not fattening. A few of these a day will have little effect on your weight. You may add them to your meals or snacks.

Small snacks:

- These snacks have 50 calories.

Medium snacks:

- These snacks have 100 calories.
- Two small snacks would equal one medium snack.

Large snacks:

- These snacks have 200 calories.
- Two medium snacks, or four small snacks, would equal one large snack.

Remember to drink water when you have a snack.
And try to avoid late night snacking.

Remember:
- *1 medium snack = 2 small snacks*

- *1 large snack = 2 medium snacks, or 4 small snacks*

Choose a variety of snacks and you won't get bored. When you eat a snack between meals you will not feel so hungry at meal times. Most of the snacks are low in fat and sugar, just like the meals. A snack made from a milk food will give you important calcium, a bran muffin will give you fiber, and a fruit is full of vitamins.

What about eating candy, chocolates and chips and other foods that are made with lots of fat or sugar? It is okay to have a small amount of these once in a while. But these shouldn't be eaten every day, as they give you calories but little nutrition. On the photographs on pages 224-229 you will find these kinds of foods marked as occasional snacks. Alcoholic drinks are also marked as an occasional snack choice. Remember the cautions about alcohol (see page 41).

In the photograph of each snack group are snacks with about the same number of calories. However, the snacks have different amounts of sugar or starch, protein or fat.

The grams of carbohydrates in each snack are listed in red.

In the small, medium and large photographs, you will find:

- starchy snacks which have mostly starch
- fruit and vegetable snacks which have natural sugar
- milk snacks have natural milk sugar and protein; and some may have some fat
- mixed snacks which are a mix of foods from different food groups, such as a starch and a protein
- occasional snacks that are high in fat or sugar, or that have alcohol.

If you have diabetes and you take insulin or a diabetes pill in the evening, read this: An evening snack that has some protein or fat may help prevent low blood sugar in the middle of the night. Ask your doctor or dietitian for more advice.

221

Low-calorie snacks
20 calories or less in each snack
Carbohydrates in grams are marked in red.

Drinks

1. water is your best low-calorie snack **0**
2. diet soft drinks and pack-aged diet drink mixes **0**
3. herbal tea **1**
4. coffee or tea **1** (regular or decaffeinated)— have your coffee or tea black or add a small amount of low-fat milk, skim milk powder or light whitener. Cut back on sugar and try a low-calorie sweetener instead.
5. bouillon or broth **4**—you may want to look for low-salt brands.

Additions to your meals or snacks

6. low-calorie sweeteners **1**
7. flavorings, such as cocoa, spices and herbs **1**
8. 1 teaspoon mustard **0**, relish **2** or ketchup **1**
9. hot sauce **0**
10. vinegar **1**
11. 1 tablespoon salsa **1**
12. 1 teaspoon honey **7**, jam, jelly or syrup **5** (diet jam or diet syrup will have less sugar)
13. 1 tablespoon bran or 1 tablespoon flaxseed (2 kinds shown) or 1–2 teaspoons ground flaxseed **2**
14. 1 tablespoon whipped or frozen topping (or 1 tablespoon of light sour cream or 2 tablespoon of fat-free sour cream) **1-2**
15. 1 tablespoon oil-free salad dressing **1-5**

222

Other Snacks

16. 1/4 cup sauerkraut **3**
17. 1 cup salad greens **1**
18. 1 soda cracker **2**
19. 1/2 cup Jellied Vegetable Salad **2** (see recipe page 139)
20. half a tomato **3**
21. 1/2 cup light gelatin **2**
22. 1 piece sugar-free gum **1** or regular gum **3**
23. 1 mint or small hard candy **4**
24. several mini-mints **2-3**
25. 1 sugar-free popsicle **5**
26. 2 green olives **0**
27. 3 radishes **1**
28. 1 dill pickle or 14 pickled hot pepper rings **2**
29. lemon and lime **4**
30. a stalk of celery **1**
31. 1/2 cucumber **3**

Small snacks

50 calories in each snack

Carbohydrates in grams are marked in red.

Vegetables

Always have raw, washed vegetables in the fridge. The vegetables should be ready-to-eat and easy to grab.

1. 3/4 cup Coleslaw (page 80) **9**
2. 1 stalk celery with 1 tablespoon cheese spread **2**
3. large salad with 1 tablespoon fat-free salad dressing **5**
4. 1 medium carrot **8**
5. 1 cup canned tomatoes **10**

Fruit

6. 1 cup of strawberries **12**
7. 1 small orange **14**
8. 1/2 large grapefruit **12**
9. 1/2 medium apple **11**
10. 1 medium plum **10**
11. 1 medium kiwi **12**
12. 2 prunes (or figs) **11**
13. 2 tablespoons raisins **16**
14. 2-inch piece of banana **13**
15. 3/4 cup Light Gelatin with Fruit (page 183) **13**
16. 3/4 cup Stewed Rhubarb (page 107) **10**

Juice

17. 1 cup tomato or vegetable juice **10**
18. 1/2 cup unsweetened fruit juice **13** (try mixing the juice with some sparkling water or diet ginger ale)

Milk snacks

19. 1/2 cup low-fat fruit yogurt sweetened with a low-calorie sweetener **8**
20. 1 cup light hot cocoa **8**
21. 1/2 cup low-fat milk (skim or 1 percent) **6**
22. 1 light fudge ice cream bar, revello or creamsicle (made with a low-calorie sweetener) **12**

Starchy snacks

23. 1 cup puffed wheat cereal **10**
24. 1 cup of packaged soup **8**
25. 2 bread sticks **8**
26. 1 rice cake **12**
27. 1 digestive cookie or other plain cookie **8**

28. 2 medium crackers **5**
29. 2 melba toast **8**
30. 4 soda crackers **9**
31. 1 fibre crispbread **7**
32. 2 Graham wafer halves **11**
33. 2 poppadums **9**

Occasional snacks

34. 1 chocolate chip cookie **7**
35. 1 fig bar **11**
36. 1/4 cup (21) fish crackers **7**
37. 3 hard candy mints **12**
38. 5 lifesavers **15**
39. a small chocolate **6**
40. 2 marshmallows **12**
41. 3 ounces dry table wine **3**

225

Medium snacks

100 calories in each snack
(two small snacks = one medium snack)
Carbohydrates in grams are marked in red.

Vegetables:

1. 2-3 cups of raw vegetables
   with 2 tablespoons of
   Vegetable Dip (page 171) **20**

Fruits

2. 1/2 medium cantaloupe **22**
3. 1 cup applesauce **28**
4. 4 pineapple rings plus
   2 tablespoon juice **24**
5. 1 small banana **27**
6. 3 figs **29**
7. 5 dried apricots **22**
8. 1 pear **25**
9. 1 cup fresh fruit salad **27**
10. 4 thin slices watermelon **22**
11. 1 1/2 cup grapes **24**

Starchy foods

12. 1 slice raisin bread
    with 1 teaspoon
    of margarine **14**
13. 3 arrowroots
    or other plain
    cookies **17**
14. 6 pretzels **24**
15. 1 waffle or
    crumpet with
    1 teaspoon jam **21**
16. 3 cups air-popped
    popcorn **19**
17. 1 whole wheat roll with
    cucumber, tomato, lettuce **19**
18. 1/3 of an 80 gram package of
    oriental noodles **20**
19. 1 slice matzo bread **27**
20. 8 baked tortilla chips or other baked chips
    with 1 tablespoon salsa sauce **12**

Mixed snacks

21. Half of a pizza bun **13**
22. 1 piece toast with 1 teaspoon peanut butter **15**
23. 1/2 cup 1 percent cottage cheese and
    1/2 tomato **6**
24. 1 cup canned tomatoes and 2 tablespoons
    shredded cheese **10**
25. 2/3 cup oat o's cereal and 1/2 cup low-fat
    milk **17**

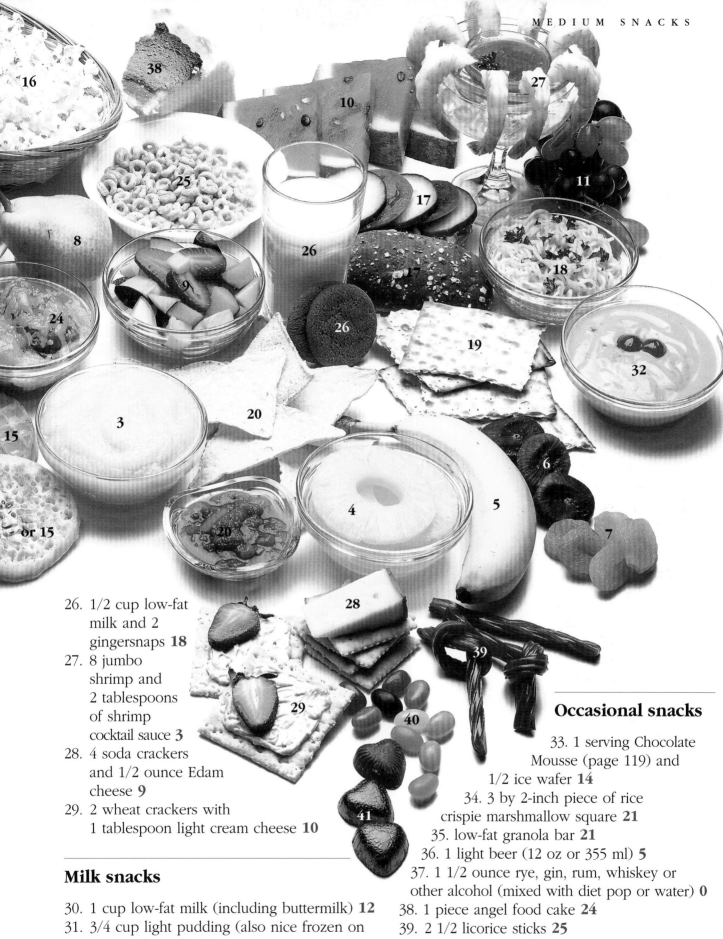

26. 1/2 cup low-fat milk and 2 gingersnaps **18**
27. 8 jumbo shrimp and 2 tablespoons of shrimp cocktail sauce **3**
28. 4 soda crackers and 1/2 ounce Edam cheese **9**
29. 2 wheat crackers with 1 tablespoon light cream cheese **10**

Milk snacks

30. 1 cup low-fat milk (including buttermilk) **12**
31. 3/4 cup light pudding (also nice frozen on a popsicle stick) **17**
32. 3/4 cup low-fat yogurt **12**

Occasional snacks

33. 1 serving Chocolate Mousse (page 119) and 1/2 ice wafer **14**
34. 3 by 2-inch piece of rice crispie marshmallow square **21**
35. low-fat granola bar **21**
36. 1 light beer (12 oz or 355 ml) **5**
37. 1 1/2 ounce rye, gin, rum, whiskey or other alcohol (mixed with diet pop or water) **0**
38. 1 piece angel food cake **24**
39. 2 1/2 licorice sticks **25**
40. 10 jelly beans **26**
41. 3 chocolate pieces (20 grams in total) **13**

Large Snacks

200 calories in each snack
(two medium snacks = one large snack)
Carbohydrates in grams are marked in red.

Mixed snacks

1. Vegetable and cracker bowl: 2 cups any kind of raw vegetables with 3 snackbreads, 2 bread sticks and 3 tablespoons Vegetable Dip (page 171). **42**
2. 2 slices toast with 1 teaspoon of butter or margarine and 2 teaspoons of jam **38**
3. 1 cup cream of wheat hot cereal and 3/4 cup low-fat milk **36**
4. 1 piece Crustless Pumpkin Pie (page 159) with 2 tablespoons whipped topping **33**
5. 1 small cone with 3/4 cup light ice cream **26**
6. 1 Bran Muffin (page 64) and 1/2 ounce cheese **29**
7. 1 piece Bannock (page 115) and 1 teaspoon jam **37**
8. 16 fresh peanuts **6**
9. 1 slice pumpernickel bread with 1 teaspoon of margarine and 1 1/2 ounces pickled herring **16**
10. 1 cup low-fat milk or buttermilk plus 3 plain cookies **30**
11. 1 cup Rice Pudding (page 111) **41**
12. large cob of corn with 1 teaspoon of butter or margarine **40**
13. small baked potato with 1 tablespoon light sour cream **47**
14. 1 Baked Apple (page 147) plus 1/2 ounce cheese **32**
15. 4 crackers with 2 large sardines **10**
16. 1/2 can cream of tomato soup made with low-fat milk, and 2 soda crackers **33**
17. 1 ounce cheese and asparagus on bread **16**
18. 1 shredded wheat with 1/2 small banana and 1/2 cup low-fat milk **45**
19. 1/2 bagel with 2 tablespoons of light cream cheese **27**

20. mixed nuts as shown **7**
21. 16 baked tortilla chips and 2 tablespoons
    of hummus or salsa **26**
22. ham sandwich (1 ounce meat,
    no margarine) with mustard and lettuce **30**
23. 1 egg and 1 toast with 1 teaspoon
    margarine (1 teaspoon jam is optional) **20**
24. 1 ounce cheese and fruit pieces **24**

Fruits

25. Two fruits, such as a small apple
    and a pear **51**
26. Half a large avocado (try with a sprinkle
    of Worcestershire sauce or lemon) **8**

Occasional snacks

27. small cake donut **23**
28. cheesies (about 25) **20**
29. potato chips (about 18) **18**
30. 40g chocolate bar **24**

Index

230

MEALS FOR Good Health

HEALTHY LIVING: Healthy living is making small changes such as walking and eating well. *Meals for Good Health* will show you how. Use this book to keep a healthy weight, to feel and look your best.

LOSING WEIGHT: Daily meal plans have the same calories, ranging from 1200-2200 calories. Losing weight is easy and fun with the delicious recipes and meals in this book because you can eat your favourite foods and snacks and lose weight at the same time. Just look at the beautiful actual-size photographs and you'll see at a glance what and how much to eat for good health.

MANAGING DIABETES: By choosing the meals and snacks shown, you can reduce your portions and carbohydrates to help bring down your blood sugars and help you lose weight. Use this guide to help prevent type 2 diabetes.

KEEPING YOUR HEART HEALTHY: Fats, cholesterol, salt and calories are reduced in the meals to promote heart health – you can lose weight if needed, reduce your levels of blood cholesterol and improve your blood pressure.

HELPING TO REDUCE YOUR RISK OF CANCER: The meals in this book are rich in vitamins and minerals. The low-fat, high-fiber meals include lots of grains, fruits and vegetables.

Karen Graham is a Registered Dietitian and Certified Diabetes Educator. For the past twenty years she has been a nutrition counselor and has specialized in helping people lose weight and in preventing and treating diabetes and heart disease.

***Meals for Good Health** is her fourth book. It was nominated for the Lieutenant Governor's Medal for Literacy and won the Dietitians of Canada Regional Speaking of Food & Eating Award: Excellence in Consumer Nutrition Communication.*